Falling for Saigon

By Connla Stokes

BRIXTON INK

First published in the United Kingdom by Brixton Ink 2025
Copyright © Connla Stokes

Connla Stokes has asserted his right under the Copyright Designs and Patents
Act 1988 to be identified as the author of this work

Several essays, or portions of some essays, in this collection are adapted from
works that were originally published (in many cases with different titles)
elsewhere: 'How to love the rainy season,' 'It's nhau or never,' 'Tet is oh so quiet'
in *VnExpress International* (online); 'Falling for Old Saigon,' 'The rest has to be
eaten,' 'Don't fence me in,' 'A nearby neighbourhood' and 'Bend with the wind'
in *Mekong Review*; 'Lost in the backstreets' in *Silverkris*, and 'Saigon's still singing'
in *Aspire* and *Travel + Leisure SEA*.

BRIXTON INK

Brixton Ink Limited Company Number 14823240
Unit 13A, 246 Stockwell Road, London, SW9 9SP, UK

Printed and bound in Great Britain by Clays Ltd Elcograf S.p.A.
A CIP catalogue record for this book is available from the British Library
ISBN 978-1-7394243-9-8

In memory of my mother, Mary.
You never made it to Saigon – I really wish you had ...

Note on language and spelling

Heads up, we have used British English spelling (although the author would prefer to call it Hiberno-English) throughout this book. A little more controversially, we have decided not to use diacritics for the small number of Vietnamese words and phrases peppered through the text. This has been done to simplify the reading experience for those who don't speak Vietnamese. After all, the tones are only useful if you speak or read the Vietnamese language, and if you don't – and the majority of those reading this book would sit in this latter category – their absence won't make any difference. We understand this will disappoint some Vietnamese speakers but we trust they will know exactly how the word is pronounced and carry on regardless.

On Vietnamese names

For those who don't know, the order of names in Vietnam is surname first, given name second. So someone called Nguyen Ha would be called Ha by her friends. To retain the friendly, conversational tone in these essays, we have stuck with Vietnamese people's 'first names' which, um, means using the last name – so my friends Tran Han and Dang Duong are referred to as Han and Duong.

On the city's names

Officially renamed Ho Chi Minh City in 1976 but still often referred to as Saigon in conversation, for many residents the city's two names are interchangeable. The text uses Ho Chi Minh City for all references post-1976 and Saigon for all references pre-1975. We have also retained the word Saigon when it was used by anyone who is quoted in the book. After all, it's their call.

'Come, sit down. Tell me about that city
you love so much.'

Tezer Özlü

Preface

'And I rose
In rainy autumn
And walked abroad in a shower of all my days.'
Dylan Thomas

Whenever I get asked why I came to Vietnam in the first place, I hesitate, because the truth is I am not really sure. I remember sitting in my friend Alan's shabby flat in Dublin. The weather was dark and dismal outside, so a fire was lit and eventually a question came to us. Should we go and live in Asia? It seemed like a solid escape plan for two fresh-faced graduates unsure of what they would do with their lives. So we started spitballing possible destinations. Alan claims that one of us held up a map of Asia while the other threw a blob of Blu Tack to determine our destination and it struck Vietnam. It sounds like a scene lifted from a film to me, but Alan swears by it. As that old John Prine song goes, there were all these things that I don't think I remember. How lucky can one man get?

Whatever sent me in the direction of Vietnam, I landed at Hanoi's Noi Bai Airport in mid-November more than twenty-five years ago with the intention of staying for a year and a bit. Slowly a life formed and I never got around to thinking about leaving Vietnam. From the very beginning, I was writing pieces about my new home; and although the following collection is focused on Ho Chi Minh City in contemporary times, these essays are all part of the same ongoing process – an attempt to describe a world for which, in the beginning, I had no words.

Besides thanking everyone who is quoted in this collection, I would like to thank every single Saigonese person and resident of Ho Chi Minh City who has ever answered a question that I have randomly thrown at them while I have been sitting in a cafe or bar, or standing by the side of a road, thinking about an essay I would like one day to finish. I am also indebted to the Saigonese journalist Pham Cong Luan who has shared so much of his work with me in the past few years. My thanks also to Tu Anh for persuading me to move to Ho Chi Minh City in the first place, my dear friend Calvin Godfrey and my father Dermot for reading so much of my writing before I shared it with the world. And last but not least, to that blob of Blu Tack, what can I say – you struck gold.

Introduction

Saigon, Ho Chi Minh City, whichever name you call it, contradicts itself. For it is large and contains multitudes. Now a sprawling and rapidly developing megacity, it has always been a meeting point for traders and a magnet for migrants, even when it was just a muddy settlement in the early eighteenth century. Since then everyone who was born here, or has come to live here, has had their own experience, their own interpretation, and their own story. This one is mine.

It was thirteen years ago when I left Hanoi, the capital of Vietnam, pretty much dragging my feet to the airport, dreading the thought of starting from scratch in another city at the other end of the country. Since the last weeks of the twentieth century, and until that point, I had been happily ensconced in Hanoi: a motley crew of wonderful friends; a steady job as the editor of a magazine; great relationships with my local colleagues; and a deep attachment to that city's dreamy aesthetics – those drowsy lakes, crumbling villas, century-old trees, centuries-old pagodas. I had all that and what's more, I knew the Vietnamese capital like the back of my hand and felt as though I had earned my stripes with the locals ten times over. Last but not least, Hanoi is where my son Caelan was born, and where his Vietnamese grandparents lived. It's his ancestral homeland, not mine, but I saw myself not only as a loyal Hanoian but a 'one-club man.' How could I even think of moving to the 'great rival,' a thousand kilometres to the south? But then, one fine spring day, when life is always full of promise for new beginnings, my ex-partner Tu Anh – a born-and-bred Hanoi girl, who was already commuting up and down the country – was asked by her employer to accept a promotion of sorts and make the southern hub a permanent base.

While living in Hanoi, I'd visited Ho Chi Minh City (nee Saigon) umpteen times, more than enough to dismiss it as 'fun for a weekend, but I wouldn't want to live there.' Every time I returned to Hanoi, I was guilty of repeating many of the cliches I had heard from locals up north. Southern food? Too sweet, too spicy; not a patch on the refined Hanoian specialties! The Saigionese lifestyle? So lazy, so decadent! And the Saigonese accent? Incomprehensible! In other words, I was a snooty northerner. But I once read a whimsical observation that for every five Hanoians that look down their nose at Ho Chi Minh City, four will move there anyway. And so, one year, I became a statistic of sorts – another turncoat who packed his bags (leaving all my scarves, beanies, and coats behind) and migrated to the winterless south.

As it happens, just a few months after I relocated, Vietnam slid into a financial crisis, triggered by the collapse of a property bubble, and accompanied by the arrest of high-level bank executives. In a sign of the times, Tu Anh was quickly reassigned from her original role (facilitating the acquisition of a major real estate development) to a taskforce dealing with toxic debt. But as a layabout man of letters in search of the easy life, none of that bothered me too much. My new place of residence felt a little roomier compared with Hanoi. The traffic felt less aggressive, the air less humid. When I went out in the evenings, I usually went to a *quan nhau* (a restaurant where locals go to eat, drink and be merry) to meet up with some fellow turncoats I had known back in the capital. We'd drink our way through a crate of bottled beer, snacking on classic southern dishes, sharing our not-so-profound insights into a city we didn't know very well. At that time, a number of unfinished high-rises loomed over the Saigon River and central thoroughfares, symbolising the real estate development inertia that had fallen on the city. Ho Chi Minh City's immediate future as a 'financial powerhouse' – as it is so often described in the international media – was looking a bit shaky. But on a superficial level, the city, with its near infinite street life, ticked over. The traffic trundled on. Bars and restaurants, so many of which spill out onto the street, appeared lively. Every second local that I met seemed to have a side business and, because it's easy to feed off the city's energy, every other foreigner I met seemed to be cooking up a scheme, too.

During my first few months, I was sometimes overwhelmed by the vastness of Ho Chi Minh City, which covers a whopping two thousand square kilometres. I remember abandoning one of my earliest crosstown trips, foolishly riding my not-so-trusty Vespa PX under a blazing midday sun wondering who would break down first – me or the Vespa. When I was caught in a deluge after a day in the saddle, I mostly felt relief. Sitting in my sodden clothes on the terrace of a French restaurant, the one that's located on the grounds of what once was a colonial opium refinery, I got talking to a Hanoian artist, another turncoat, who kindly explained what I could expect from the city's two seasons: 'Six months of people complaining about how it's getting hotter, and hotter, and *hotter*, followed by six months of people complaining about how much it's raining.' From the beginning, I struggled when using my intermediate-level Vietnamese as I was more familiar with the Hanoian accent and dialect. In Ho Chi Minh City, one minute you might be talking to a woman from the Mekong Delta in the southwest of Vietnam next you'd find yourself trying to communicate with a taxi driver from Hue in north central Vietnam. I persevered as best I could, but looking back at that period now, I can see how I was needlessly seeking Hanoi, and guilty of trying to assert my Hanoian credentials in Ho Chi Minh City, when I might have been better off letting go. I searched for restaurants that prepared *pho* and *bun cha* (noodles with barbecued pork) for the northern palette. I even looked out for restaurants serving *bia hoi* – the cheap fresh beer beloved by northerners but which is far from ubiquitous in the south. One night, I sat at Pho Ha, a street-side restaurant known for its Hanoian-style chicken *pho*, and where I quickly realised I *could* understand much of the banter around me. They were all northerners, also pining for the taste of home. Southern comfort for northern souls, I guess.

Attending a wedding during my first year in Ho Chi Minh City, I met some of Tu Anh's Saigonese cousins, who all playfully teased me over my rigid northern tones and reassured me I would eventually grow to love Saigonese food (they weren't wrong). This branch of a rather complex family tree was in the south because Tu Anh's mother's half-sister had migrated south with her husband (a pharmacist), right after the Geneva Accords divided Vietnam at the Seventeenth Parallel following the Vietnamese victory over French colonial forces in Dien Bien Phu, now more than seventy years ago. At the wedding, I met the long-deceased aunt's son-in-law, who was in his late sixties but seemed much older. As soon as he clocked me, he made it clear to everyone that I would be sitting beside him. At first, I figured he was just keen to shoot the breeze in English with a foreigner, but he had his own story, which began with him telling me he had chosen to stay in Saigon at the end of the American-Vietnam war. His wife had been working at the US embassy as a secretary and so she could have at least tried to get them evacuated on one of the helicopters, the 'Jolly Green Giants,' as they were known – the ones that sent the whole city into a panic when they corkscrewed out through thunder clouds the day before a divided Vietnam was reunified in 1975. He told me that he stayed because he was Saigonese and didn't want to live anywhere else (something I now understand very well), but it was evident that he had regrets. As the evening wore on, he became a bit 'tired and emotional' as the old euphemism goes, and eventually, his wife, who hadn't let on that she even spoke English, discreetly suggested I should go check on my son, a fractious toddler in those days. I took the hint and scooched down the table.

It is now fifty years since that man made his decision to stay. Fifty years since the war finally ended. Fifty years since the sound of the last American choppers departed and didn't look back. And fifty years since a reunified Vietnam came into being. Even then Saigon was full of contradictions. For it was large and contained multitudes. Whoever was there that day had their own experiences, and now, if still alive, they have their own interpretation of the events, and their own story. Some Saigonese with connections to the Americans got to leave in the helicopters. Some didn't make the cut and later took their chances on the high seas. Some left with the choppers but, while sitting in a dusty refugee camp, asked if they could be brought back. Those who stayed in the city reacted in different ways. Some went into hiding. Some went looting. Some wondered what people in the north liked to eat (rice, of course). And some brought tea out into the streets for the northern soldiers who had just taken control of the city but, like everyone else, were unsure what would happen next. What followed is a complicated period of history that has been told many times from different perspectives. All I will say is that ultimately the Saigonese spirit endured. The easy-going, fun-loving, hospitable locals that you will meet in the city's numerous neighbourhoods today are a testament to the intangible, infectious and ineradicable charm of the people in this city, a city which continues to welcome newcomers today, some of whom are like me, but many of whom are nothing like me. If we – the multitudes with all our contradictions – share one thing, it's that the song of Saigon has captured our hearts. Because when you fall for this city and its way of life, you can easily think, as I do now, that there is nowhere else you would rather be.

*

It's not that I don't have moments of frustration living here. Because I do. Perhaps when I am caught in the searing sunshine, staring at a never-ending torrent of vehicles as far as the eye can see. Sometimes that's all you see in this city. *Traffic.* It might be 2pm and, not for the first time, an enervating heat has drained me. As I walk, sounds can bombard my jittery senses. Why, I might think, must a newly opened bakery play pumping techno from mounted speakers that face the street? And as I press on, I will likely hear the honks of a hundred thousand bikes, beeping in blithe indifference to it all. At times on the pavement of one thoroughfare or another, I feel like I have to shout to be heard. But every time, Ho Chi Minh City, Saigon, whatever you wish to call it, wins me over again. A day that seemed too long begins to fade. The heat subsides. And soon, I know, I will find myself in a cosy cafe, a neighbourhood restaurant, or a hidden bar, somewhere where I have everything I need – a good vibe, good food, and good company (even if I am alone). And if anything, the more time goes by, the more I have learned to appreciate being in that 'happy place,' wherever it is, and whoever I am with. Because you don't have to live in Ho Chi Minh City for very long to realise how quickly things can change. It's far from unusual to discover something you cherish has disappeared overnight, and you can easily find yourself getting nostalgic about the way things used to be, you know, like, last Tuesday. But I find that the trick, if there is one, is to stay curious and keep exploring, to keep starting new conversations, and to keep discovering the stories of others who call this city home. Whenever I do that, I find that the pleasure of finding new places and meeting new people in this city never gets old. Because, in the end, whether you ask for them or not, isn't life always about new beginnings?

EAT
OUT

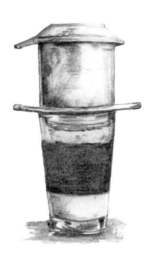

The rest has to be eaten

'You don't have to go looking for great food in
Vietnam. Great food finds you.'

Anthony Bourdain

I can't say what makes each of us fall in love with
Vietnamese food. It might have been a thousand
and one different things. A nourishing fix of *pho* you
slurped down at dawn (at midnight, after one too
many beers). The first time you grabbed a pair of
chopsticks and tossed a bowl of *com hen* (a rice salad
with basket clams, fried pork skin, peanuts and herbs)
and dug in. Or maybe when you dunked a crusty *banh
mi* into a zesty beef stew laced with lemongrass, or
hoovered up a comforting plate of *com ga* (chicken

on rice). Or perhaps it was an artery-clogging, still-sizzling-in-oil steak served with eggs and pate that turned your head? I would happily wax lyrical about the first time I ate a chilled, perfectly ripe mango – a revelatory experience for an Irishman raised eating tropical fruits from a tin.

What can I say? It all gets under your skin. The colours, flavours, textures, sounds, situations. The heat and humidity? You won't notice it once you start eating. You won't even care that your shirt is straightaway a sodden rag, not when you're devouring what might be the greatest noodle soup of its kind in the universe, or devouring a table-load of tasty morsels, all washed down with whatever local brew is to hand, wondering if this gastronomic joy is as good as gets ...

However or whenever it happens, just as Thomas Fowler in Graham Greene's *The Quiet American* said (okay, fine, he wasn't *actually* referring to the food), there comes a point for many of us when we realise that we have come to Vietnam and nothing can ever be the same again. Where were you when you felt it, this ... *awakening*? Perhaps, like me, you only realised you'd been altered on a trip home, when you found yourself getting claustrophobic in a restaurant of the most generic, international kind – staff in head-to-toe black clobber, music set to ambient, menus, wine lists, napkins, conventions, formality – and you couldn't help feeling insulted by a life-long friend proclaiming, nose in menu, 'I'm having the T-bone steak, what are *you* having?' In this instant, you saw the restaurant for what it was: a business, an investment, a cold, calculated move to tap a market, and you longed for the ease of eating out at the fuss-free, family-run street-side eateries of Saigon, from which there are tens of thousands to choose.

Because it's not just the food, it's also the context. It's the informality of it, the buoyant spirit of the place. It's who you are with, and how they're looking at you. And even if you are on your own, you're never alone in these entertainingly overstaffed restaurants, where the owners are always on hand. They welcome you, and sometimes even cook for you, and consistently, day in, day out, year after year, they nail it. Sure, be my guest, go check out the new Italian or Spanish place that seems to have confused itself with a nightclub, or whatever high-end fusion joint is in vogue for taking you (and your wallet) on a *very* expensive, culinary journey. But don't tell me it *changed* anything for you.

Although I first stepped into the light in Hanoi, where I was introduced to the basics of Vietnamese cuisine, and developed a taste for the fresh herbs and fermented flavours, I think Ho Chi Minh City has the edge when it comes to eating out. No, *wait,* I don't mean it's *better.* No shots have been fired. No controversy has been stoked. But for me, the diversity of Ho Chi Minh City – Vietnam's only true melting pot – makes it one of the world's greatest cities for food. Where else can you eat a hundred different noodle soups at any time of the day or night? Or find specialities from every regional hub in the country – Hue, Hoi An, Danang, Nha Trang, Hanoi, Dalat, Can Tho, Quy Nhon ... they're all here in numbers. And if you ever get bored of straight-up Vietnamese cuisine in Ho Chi Minh City, you can lose yourself among the crowds of Cholon (an area commonly referred to as Chinatown, which sprawls across the western side of the city) for an endless array of localised Chinese staples – char siew wanton noodles, dim sum, egg noodles with steamed duck, crackling pork, salted egg custard buns, or sticky rice with coconut cream and durian.

Will you also see a thousand and one fast food outlets and international franchises competing for your attention with gaudy signs and flashing lights? Of course, you will – because the city also has a great appetite for foreign foods, and that's nothing new. But the majority of food fads come and go while most franchises tend to fizzle. And the Vietnamese people's profound love of their own cuisine? That, my friends, is eternal.

*

Long before it became popular around the world, the biggest evangelist for Vietnamese cuisine was the late Anthony Bourdain. Rewatching his old shows produced in Vietnam, it seems clear to me that he was happiest when not forced to intellectualise too much; to simply be sitting on a Lilliputian plastic chair, eating something (he's not sure exactly what) with well-used chopsticks, in a place where nobody cares about grimy walls, or litter-strewn floors, because the food is just too bloody good. As he returned to Ho Chi Minh City in subsequent years and noted the rapid changes, including the rise of western franchises, Bourdain might easily have bought into the narrative that locals were increasingly falling under the spell of shitty foreign foods.

Sure, if we sent a Fowler to report on Ho Chi Minh City today, and asked him to look into the present state of Vietnamese street food and family-run eateries, he might come away with a fairly grim view, especially if he wandered out of Greene's favourite hotels, the Majestic or the Continental, and strolled along the pedestrianised Nguyen Hue Boulevard, which runs from the Saigon River to the Ho Chi Minh City People's Committee Building. They're all there now, those symbols of homogenised doom: the Golden Arches, the Starbucks mermaid, a host of other fast-food outlets, and generic international restaurants.

But if someone coaxed the old bean out of his bubble and into the fringes of District 1 or beyond, where so much of the city is still a riot of old-school, al fresco, informal dining, what would strike him? The smell: that'd be the first thing to hit him, promising everything in exchange for his soul. The heat? He'd just have to ignore it. His shirt? Yes, straightaway a rag. And soon he would hardly remember his name, or what it was he came to escape, because he has just been served a plate of *com tam* ('broken rice' with a grilled pork chop, a sort of frittata, a fried egg with a runny yolk and pickles), or a bowl of *bun ca* (a soup of fine rice noodles, a chunk of fresh fish, fish cake, and a hedgerow of herbs) and after one glorious, mind-blowing, life-altering mouthful, we would be able to forgive him for not caring what the future may bring. Because it's still true that you can come to Vietnam and learn a lot in the first few minutes. But the rest? It has to be eaten.

It's nhau
or never ...

In Ho Chi Minh City, and other parts of Vietnam, when somebody says it's time for a *nhau* (see glossary), it's a clarion call to go drinking and feasting – not that the word solely means 'to go drinking and feasting.' There's more to it than that.

Many moons ago, I recall a man from Danang – a city in Central Vietnam – telling a friend of mine that *nhau* meant 'eating and drinking for no particular purpose.' But, as all Vietnamese folk reading this will know, there *is* a purpose (other than eating and drinking) – one that involves life-affirming pleasures, such as spontaneous socialisation, the trading of banter, the teasing of peers, the cracking of jokes, the sound of someone bursting into song; all performed joyously in the key of camaraderie.

I guess what the man from Danang meant was that no one has to be celebrating a birthday, and it doesn't have to be a national holiday – or even the end of the week. It can be a run-of-the-mill Tuesday evening when somebody decides they want to eat, drink and be merry, and that somebody needs company: siblings, uncles, aunts, nephews, nieces and cousins; a gang of friends; a bunch of colleagues; neighbours; teammates; classmates (new or old) ... whomever. Without much notice, they will be summoned and a *nhau* will begin.

If some western readers think this sounds like the Vietnamese equivalent of after-work drinks, or heading down the local pub with a gang of mates, you're underestimating the importance of feasting. Even if they plan to get plastered, nobody in Vietnam cares to imbibe without food of some description on the table. When people convene for a *nhau*, a venue may be selected for the quality of its grub rather than a convenient location (forget TripAdvisor – in a sprawling city famed for its congested roads, if someone rides a scooter for eight kilometres to a particular eatery, the owner should feel free to brag).

Now, for the uninitiated, some additional pointers:

it only takes two to *nhau*, but three's better; and a simple rule of thumb: the more the merrier. Also, no one braves the crosstown traffic to *nhau* in a fancy restaurant – too stiff, too stuffy; too alienating for those unacquainted with fine-dining conventions. Nor can you *nhau* at a noodle joint, where you're expected to slurp your bowl down and skedaddle to make way for the next hungry punter.

For optimal *nhau* conditions, you need an airy space, plenty of time and, above all else, a feeling of freedom. Every table should feel like they can stay as long as they want, drink as much as they want, sing, and laugh, and shout as loud as they want. For that reason most Saigonese prefer going to an old school *quan nhau* (see glossary), a tavern of sorts, preferably one that spills out onto a pavement, where they will be seated in plastic chairs at fold-up tables and presented with a single, exhaustive menu. Each venue may have its own specialties but the ensuing feast is invariably heavy on protein and light on carbs (rice would only rob room for beer).

As the evening unfolds, each dish lands without ceremony in the middle of the table. The commensal spirit of such gatherings is innate to Vietnamese. No one orders their own steak-frites or the catch of the day. Every participant is part of a chorus. They eat and drink and laugh as one.

There are also no individual orders of beer, and no trace of any fancy IPAs – it's one commercial beer or another for the whole table. After a crate has been dragged to the table, cylinders of ice are placed in glasses, even if the bottles have been refrigerated. Sacrilege? Elsewhere in the world, sure, but in Ho Chi Minh City: a) the ice keeps the beer cold in spite of the soupy heat; and b) if challenged to knock it back in one, even a beer snob can warm to the virtues of a watery beer in a glass that's 33 per cent ice.

In parts of Saigon, a busker might wander past the most popular *quan nhau*, strumming as he strolls, hoping a table of nostalgic revellers will coo him over to croon a sentimental ballad in exchange for tips. But with or without music, come 9pm, the best *quan nhau* will have an infectious air of festivity. Flustered staff will be run off their feet until every table has had its fill of food, beer, gossip and stories.

Which brings us to the final act of the night: settling the bill. Invariably, someone will seize it and make a gallant attempt to pay for everyone, but the rest of the table will often protest. Let's all chip in, someone might reason, and do this again soon.

And they surely will – later that month, or even the following week; whenever somebody wants to eat, drink and be merry, and that somebody needs company.

The cafe society

When visiting his father at a public hospital in Ho Chi Minh City some years ago, Pham Cong Luan, a Saigonese memoirist and journalist, heard the anguished cries of another patient, an elderly fellow who'd had a stroke. At the end of his tether, the ailing man wailed at the doctor and nurses: 'Let me go home and drink coffee!'

'Most Saigonese people, whether rich or poor, like to start the day with coffee, but we rarely drink it in our *actual* home,' Luan told me later. 'This man really wanted to be back in his local alleyway, chit-chatting with friends while sipping on a *ca phe sua da*. (See glossary)'

Wherever this man lived in the city, his local cafe would likely have been his 'third place'. His playroom. His living room. His observation post. Somewhere to be with his mates and kill an hour or three, watching life roll by and speaking of how things used to be. As Bui Giang, a beloved twentieth-century Vietnamese poet, once wrote of Saigon: 'A small cafe in the alley feels like home'. Arriving as a migrant back in the 1950s, when central Saigon still had the feel of a French provincial town (just a very tropical one), Giang would have been served a coffee with a metal drip filter placed over a glass. Watching the caffeinated liquid trickle through to the ice below would have been part of the pleasure. Because drinking coffee the old school Saigonese way meant whiling away time, not worrying about it.

Since then the same city has morphed into a heavily motorised and fast-paced hub with far less time for drip filters – today there are nearly ten million people living in the city, and if hardly anyone drinks coffee at home, just how many cafes might there be? 'There's no data for that and, honestly, I can't even guess!' said one industry insider, Tran Han, a three-time national barista champion of Vietnam (a country second only to Brazil for coffee production). 'It's partly because cafes here open and shut so quickly.

But many neighbourhood cafes in the backstreets are operating out of living rooms, or just doorways. They're not registered businesses, so no one knows how many there are.'

Even if a first-time visitor sticks to the wider boulevards of District 1, passing French colonial-period landmarks, like the Saigon Opera House and Notre Dame Cathedral, as well as the towers which are redefining the city's skyline, they would quickly lose count of the cafes they see (and let's not get started on the bubble tea phenomenon). They would also notice that the more popular commercial spots with prime pavement frontage are gathering points for Saigonese right through the evening, in some cases, till midnight.

And should you stick around any lively cafe, even if you can't follow the conversations, you'll see that locals aren't just whiling away the time – they will be there to strike a business deal, negotiate a property lease, purchase a piece of land, talk shop with colleagues, pitch to a client, check their stocks, conduct an interview, play video games, meet a loan shark, or talk loudly about startups and cryptocurrency. In some of the more photogenic cafes (very much designed to attract the Instagram/TikTok crowd), you may come across a parade of fashionistas (amateur and professional, but mostly amateur), all dressed up to the nines and taking turns to pose for photos while the iced drinks they ordered melt in the background.

At the other end of the spectrum, if you roam the city's less central districts late at night, you will find 24-hour cafes, where migrant workers – delivery men, cooks, street cleaners, taxi drivers, *xe om* (see glossary) and cyclo riders, all of those who do their bit to keep the cogs of this colossal city turning through the night – combat weariness with caffeine (or cheap energy drinks) while staring into their phones (very possibly watching TikTok videos and wondering if that's really how the other half lives).

An affable middle-aged fellow called Binh once told me that he ran such a cafe for years. Before retiring, he used to serve between sixty and a hundred iced coffees to working class men from midnight to 6am every night in the front room of his house, which is tucked away down a typical back street in the north of the city. When I asked if he went to bed after the last sleep-deprived customer finally left, Binh grinned: 'No, I'd go for coffee with my friends in the alleyway.' And should you ask any Saigon barista what they do on their day off, I bet you a cold brew they will say they go to meet friends at a coffee shop. You see, it's not because everyone in this city is addicted to caffeine. They're hooked on cafes.

Without plan or design, it's not a stretch to say that cafes have even added to Ho Chi Minh City's tourism appeal. Visitors (both domestic and international)

flock to a once-shabby but now gentrified nine-storey block of apartments on the central thoroughfare of Nguyen Hue, where you will also find a statue of Ho Chi Minh flanked by shops for luxury fashion brands and a Rolls Royce showroom. Once a purely residential building, where US military officers lived in the 1960s, 42 Nguyen Hue has become one of the city's most Instagrammed destinations thanks to its distinctive facade, adorned with neon lights and signs that advertise each of the umpteen cafes inside (there are also boutiques and restaurants throughout the building).

Whether they're escaping the scorching heat of the dry season, or a monsoonal downpour, weary tourists will quickly find themselves spending plenty of time in one cafe or another as they tour the town. The vibrant cafe scene is also a major draw for anyone who travels the world working from a laptop. And yet, even though cafe culture is evidently such a huge part of the city's DNA, the head-scratching abundance of coffee shops makes it a tough industry for investors at all levels.

In the middle of last year's rainy season, when the daily storms felt more turbulent and more unpredictable than ever, I met a business investor who expressed a weary pessimism about the cafe market that he and his consortium had hoped to crack. 'This city is a battleground for cafe chains,' he admitted while we waited for a downpour to pass.

'When everyone takes a little bit of the pie, there's no winner.'

In such a fiercely competitive and diverse cafe-scape, it has come as no surprise for insiders to see international brands struggling. Last year the city's sole Starbucks Reserve outlet closed – a billion dong (about US$40,000) in monthly revenue couldn't justify the mind-boggling US$30,000 rent they were paying. Plus, competition is fierce. Spacious cafes (with perfect WiFi, friendly staff and excellent coffee) are two a penny; and if you're minding your pennies, an iced coffee made with cheap robusta beans can cost as little as 15,000 dong (US$0.60). If you want to fork out for a V60 filter with high-end arabica beans from Central Vietnam (or imported from wherever), you're still spoilt for choice. Anyone who lives here could quite easily go to a different (and very decent) coffee shop every day of the year. We can even find a cafe to suit every mood, including fatigue: *cafe vong* ('hammock cafes'), often found in the city's outskirts, are aimed at weary commuters and long-haul drivers who have travelled from distant provinces. Squirrelled away on the higher floors of old shophouses, you might find a 'library cafe' targeting bibliophiles, or a vintage cafe with retro tunes and throwback stylings. Cat cafes, live music cafes, art cafes, garden cafes, riverside cafes, rooftop cafes, a cafe with upside down furniture. They're all around town, too, meaning everyone can find a place to call their own. As an overly caffeinated writer I have spent countless hours in countless cafes, and I am forever finding new ones to love. Not so long ago, I wandered down a narrow alley (pedestrian and motorcyclist access only) near Le Van Tam Park and found a mellow neighbourhood cafe that had a collection of vinyl records and low-tables, more suited to chit-chatting than working. When I stepped inside, I was surprised to hear the crooning voice of Leonard Cohen, whose music always reminds me of my mother pottering around the family kitchen in Dublin and humming along (because she couldn't hold a note) to 'So Long, Marianne,' and so, in this colossal city, I sat down in a little cafe that felt like home.

Don't fence me in

At one point during the Covid-19 pandemic, anyone flying into Vietnam had to do a fifteen-day quarantine. Normally I'd have regular visitors passing through the city, but for a year – or was it more? – I had none at all. One day I heard from a good friend of mine who was relocating from Bangkok to Danang. After flying into Ho Chi Minh City, she was holed up in a hotel facing the Saigon River, where for fifteen days and fifteen nights, she sat visualising freedom and imagining everything she would eat when released back into the wild. Minutes before she was due to resurface, she sent me a text: 'Let's go for lunch right *now*. I'm ravenous. Something local, something delicious, and please, choose somewhere *outdoors*.'

So under a hazy sun we strolled from the Saigon River toward the historic Rex Hotel, which was built nearly a century ago, although it was originally an automobile showroom for Citroën. In more recent times, the side entrance of the hotel used to face a high, blue metal fence with a sign that read: SORRY FOR THIS INCONVENIENCE.

Some stretches of the fencing had been a fixture for more than seven years. It went up when work on a metro line began underneath Le Loi Boulevard, a wide and long artery that runs for about 900 metres from the Saigon Opera House to Ben Thanh Market. The fencing was there so long that I had forgotten what life on Le Loi used to be like. The pandemic – another grand old inconvenience – had made it even harder for restaurants, cafes and other small businesses along the strip to survive. Unsurprisingly, many didn't make it.

In places, the fencing, which is now long gone, ran so close to the shophouses you had to shuffle sideways when passing other pedestrians. It certainly wasn't for claustrophobes, but I regularly plunged down that singular passageway to get to one of my favourite street food joints located right at the beginning of Nguyen Trung Truc (a street named after a nineteenth-century fisherman-turned-revolutionary who masterminded the burning of a French naval ship). It's the kind of place where you don't have to order (unless you're picky) because there's only one dish. Just park your backside on a plastic stool and soon you'll be handed a noodle salad with chunks of charcoal-grilled pork, a handful of herbs, some shredded carrot and daikon, a sprinkling of peanuts and a single spring roll packed with wood ear mushrooms, pork and onion, all of which gets doused with a fish-sauce-heavy dressing that's sweetened with sugar, spiced with chillies and sharpened with a solitary pickled shallot. I usually have to resist the temptation to order a second serve; if I have an appetite, I just ask for an extra spring roll or an extra skewer of pork.

No one used to believe me that such a sublime bowl of *bun thit nuong cha gio* could still be found so centrally in Ho Chi Minh City. Fearing my friend would also be sceptical, after we emerged from 'the blue fence passageway,' I first took her over to the gnarled grill, knowing that one waft of pork-scented smoke would win her over.

We took a minute to watch the family and their staff assemble bowl after bowl with their backs to a century-old building that has a little-known claim to fame. It was here, in 1929, that thirty comrades founded the Communist Party of Annam, which later merged with the Indochinese Communist Party to form the Communist Party of Vietnam. There's no plaque on the facade to mark that historic summit, just a few stickers advertising various food delivery apps, a digital disruption that was, in Covid times, a much-needed boon for lunchtime trade. By noon, in those days, there would be a queue of delivery guys impatiently waiting for orders to be bagged and bound in a knot of plastic. But I would try not to look at that. Nothing kills the mood more than the sight of street food being placed in a styrofoam box.

Thanks to the blue fence, that section of Nguyen Trung Truc Street was effectively a cul de sac, so it was pleasingly free of honking vehicles. I'd almost have described the atmosphere as serene. That day, my friend and I ate on the opposite side of the road, under the shade of camphor trees and alongside another tall, blue metal fence. This other 'temporary' perimeter, which still stands, conceals a whopping 3,800 square-metre plot of land that had been earmarked for a project, some sort of glassy, high-rise office and retail tower. I told my friend a groundbreaking ceremony was held years ago but ever since it had been a vacant lot. A number of trees inside have now grown to be much higher than the fence. One day, I suppose the fence will come down and construction will begin. And the trees? Maybe they'll stick them in a tree museum, then charge the people a dollar and a half to see them, as the old Joni

Mitchell song goes.

But that afternoon, my friend and I weren't too worried about what the future would bring. We were in the moment, eating mostly in silence, each of us too intent on enjoying every mouthful to get a dialogue going.

It was only when she had demolished the contents of her bowl that a penny dropped: 'You know, I think I ordered delivery from this place during my quarantine, but man, it wasn't nearly as tasty.' Street food ordered online? Surely that's a convenience too far. But the good news is that the next time my friend comes to visit, I'll be able to take her into town on the Metro, which belatedly opened last December to jubilant scenes twelve years after construction began. As some old prophet once said: 'Hope deferred makes the heart ache, but a desire fulfilled is a tree of life.'

Bend with the wind

Some summers ago, I was back home in Dublin for a few weeks and sitting in the family kitchen when my father found some half-forgotten *banh trang* (Vietnamese rice papers) tucked behind mason jars of arborio and basmati in the cupboard.

Rediscovering this forgotten gift from the east, and without consulting anyone in the west, he set about preparing what he called *goi cuon* (often translated as 'summer rolls,' but more accurately 'salad rolls').

In Ho Chi Minh City, through the transparent exterior of each fat yet elegantly wrapped roll, you will usually find two or three peeled prawns, a slice of boiled pork belly, two clumps of *bun* (soft rice noodles), a piece of lettuce, a few leaves of Vietnamese basil, and a single, uncut chive running up the middle and sticking out the end, like a green fuse.

Perhaps, half-confusing *goi cuon* with *banh trang phoi suong* – a Mekong Delta dish of DIY-rolls made from an extravagance of ingredients – my father riffed on food memories from multiple peregrinations to Vietnam while improvising with whatever he had to hand. He baked mackerel and salmon fillets; he shredded lettuce and sliced cucumbers; he plucked mint and picked just-ripened tomatoes from his garden; he boiled up some thin (made-in-China) noodles and fashioned a dip out of (Thai) fish sauce. Soon, the whole Stokes clan was gathered around this improvised smorgasbord and concocting slapdash rolls, most of which fell apart as they met their makers' mouths. No matter (ever tried, ever failed): the meal was declared a success in Dublin. But, I wondered what on earth a Vietnamese foodie, or, gulp, a combustible gatekeeper of Vietnamese cuisine would make of this abomination, if just one photo were to be leaked into the toxic waters of social media …

'Well, to my mind the fundamentals of Vietnamese [cuisine] are freshness and fermentation as well as improvisation – your father's summer rolls had all of these elements, but what I like about this story is that the idea travelled and inspired others,' says Hien Ngo, a US-trained biochemist turned cafe owner. For a period at his cafe Red Door, Hien used to reconfigure classic Vietnamese dishes, or 'dishes as ideas,' as their own postmodernist alter-ego selves. He had the misfortune of being a little ahead of his time with his playful and delicious culinary creations. 'Whether we know it or not,' Hien told me, 'food is always a cross section of culture.'

Instead of telling Hien that your average Irish man knows *exactly* what he's talking about (please be upstanding and salute the lasagne sandwich), I told him I was reading *Rice and Baguette: A History of Food in Vietnam* but unfortunately it doesn't include a part where a man in Ireland has a bash at making *goi cuon*, or explain why people like Hien are freely tinkering with the Vietnamese canon. The book's publication also didn't have the timing to capture how acting US president Barack Obama had a dinner date with Anthony Bourdain in Hanoi. They famously ate the capital's most popular lunchtime noodle dish, *bun cha*, at 8pm – an event that single-handedly introduced the split shift at all central Hanoi *bun cha* restaurants while also underlining that the most effective way to win 'hearts and minds' in Vietnam is to simply pull up a plastic stool and eat among the locals.

In *Rice and Baguette*, author Vu Hong Lien writes that if 'modern Vietnamese food had a voice, it would be bilingual for it is the offspring of a marriage of convenience between a rice-based culture and a wheat-based diet,' and that today's Vietnamese cuisine is a 'mix of Vietnamese and French dishes.' She admits this is a startling statement that will offend anyone who suggests that 'Vietnam's culinary culture is subject to the palate of its Chinese big brother.' Having lived in Ho Chi Minh City for well over a decade, I see it quite differently.

The effect of France unloading its pantries into Vietnamese kitchens is as undeniable as the impact of roughly ten centuries of Chinese influence (in all cultural spheres), but the 'voice' of Vietnamese cuisine isn't even trilingual. It is itself, just as the Vietnamese language is entirely Vietnamese, even if it has borrowed and absorbed much from other vocabularies (some more than others, obviously).

The heritage expert William S. Logan once wrote that Vietnam's cultural (and national) survival has depended on a Vietnamese ability to 'bend with the wind.' Concerning himself mainly with architecture, he pointed to the multi-layered urban tapestries of Hanoi and Ho Chi Minh City, which he said could be read like palimpsests of sorts.

Could we also describe Vietnamese cuisine as similarly multi-layered? If so, *Rice and Baguette* certainly succeeds in peeling away many of the layers, gamely beginning at the bottom. In Nghe An province, archaeologists once unearthed mounds of eight thousand-year-old molluscs, 'several metres high, hundreds of square metres in area' – which sounds a lot like what you'd also find on the floor of a huge oc (shellfish) restaurant in Ho Chi Minh City today, where locals feast on snails, periwinkles, scallops, cockles and mussels like there's no tomorrow.

The book also manages to capture a sense of how important Vietnamese food is to Vietnamese people, even if we're just talking about a bowl of rice. 'Over the centuries,' writes Lien, 'it had become ingrained in the Vietnamese psyche that no matter what, a meal must be hot and served with rice.' In one of the book's best anecdotes, Lien explains that when fighting the French halfway through the twentieth century, Viet Minh soldiers couldn't bear to eat cold rice, which had been cooked at night to avoid the attention of the enemy. They devised a cooking system that emitted smoke far from where the stove sat. Ultimately, the author suggests this innovation played a key role in the decisive 1954 battle of Dien Bien Phu. So if you are ever discussing this historic military battle, don't forget to mention an inventive cook from Hoa Binh called Hoang Cam deserves his own statue. Indeed, his hidden 'double stove' continued to serve Vietnamese soldiers during the American-Vietnam war. As one veteran later recalled: 'We always dug up a Hoang Cam stove to cook food. No smoke by day, no light by night. The US recon aircraft OV-10 could not detect us.' And even today, cadets joining the military for the first time will learn how to dig into the earth and build a double stove to cook for up to sixty of their comrades.

Rice and Baguette also explains how imported technology played its part in the evolution of Vietnamese cuisine. The arrival of the rice cooker, for example, in the seventies and eighties, bought home cooks more prep time for crafting dishes. Science also got in the mix – monosodium glutamate became so commonly used in Vietnam over the years it could be described as a traditional ingredient. And through the book there are also shout-outs for (in no particular order) Vietnam's cross-border and international relations with the Khmer, the Cham, the Americans, Japanese, Soviet Russians, oh, and the Romans (in the first century AD, they also had fish sauce (*garum*) – culinary wormhole theorists, you have the floor), all of which makes me think we should be wary of any simplified narratives when trying to fathom the DNA of Vietnamese cuisine.

With all this talk of absorbing foreign influences, let's not forget to hail the ingenuity of Vietnamese home-cooks and chefs, who, generation to generation, and mostly anonymously, continue both to honour culinary traditions and also adapting, tweaking and inventing dishes, forever inspired by the bounty of foodstuffs at their disposal.

During my time living in Hanoi, I noticed small evolutions in classic dishes. Responding to calls from hungry (and increasingly affluent) punters, *bun rieu* (a noodle soup with tomato, tofu and crab) stalls seemed to offer an increasing array of protein add-ins (beef, prawns, sausage ...). And when I arrived in the capital there was no such thing as *pho cuon* (sheets of pho wrapped around beef and herbs) but now it's seen as a 'traditional' street food dish (just a very young one).

Of course, as entrepreneurs search for the next food fad, some creations are not always worth celebrating. In Ho Chi Minh City, I have tried a 'rice burger' (rice 'buns', pork patties), various attempts at a *pho* burger (better to not visualise it), and even a *banh mi pho* – a sandwich that's meant to taste like the beef noodle soup? Well, not for me, but no one in Ho Chi Minh City got worked up about it.

Meanwhile, in the United Kingdom and the United States, judging by the food sections of major magazines and newspapers, there tend to be two approaches to Vietnamese food: the first encourages authenticity (e.g. 'How to cook perfect *pho*'); the second says, let's take the idea of a dish and then see what's in the supermarket/fridge. For example, one recipe that I found for *bun cha*, normally made with pork, was made – look away, ye purists – with prawn patties and lemongrass.

But therein lies the rub. When a cuisine jumps the fence, it's not just a story of exportation and replication, which is more often than not impossible – some would probably argue you can't get a worthwhile bowl of the Hoi An speciality *cao lau* five kilometres down the road in Danang. But what better gift to the world than to inspire other culinary traditions, or to change individualised perceptions of what we eat, and *how* we eat?

All of which sort of takes us back to my father's rather fishy *goi cuon*. Or, maybe I should have told you about the time he invented 'festive *pho*' from leftover turkey bones a day or two after Christmas one year? It wasn't a great success without access to fresh *pho*. But no matter – ever tried, ever failed. And you get my point. The 'idea' of Vietnamese food is travelling, more than ever before, and today, wherever you are, it's there to inspire. So I say run with it – and have fun with it. And if a photo does get out, and a combustible gatekeeper blows a gasket at the sight of your culinary abomination, just tell them to go bend with the wind.

STAY
OUT

A nearby neighbourhood

A few years back, someone messaged me on Instagram: 'Is Phuong ['Ward'] 19 in Binh Thanh district your 'hood, too?'

I had to check Google Maps. It wasn't. Technically my 'hood is Phuong 22 – a newly developed urban realm composed primarily of generic high-rise towers and a hectare's worth of *Truman Show*-style villas. For a 'corner shop,' I have nothing but convenience stores: 7/11, FamilyMart, CircleK. That's why, especially in the evening, I'm more keen to be associated with Phuong 19, a much older, more 'Saigonese' part of Ho Chi Minh City.

Not that all of it is all that old.

Some of the most eye-catching buildings in the ward are a bunch of apartment blocks named after a mid-nineteenth century mandarin scholar called Pham Viet Chanh. Built in the mid-1990s, but already seeming much older, they're not really much to look at. But architecture isn't the draw, not for me anyway. When the day is done, I walk or cycle over here just to drink in the giddy feel of the place: the street-side banter, the clinking of glasses, the laughter, the sense of community – compared to the sobering, sanitised surroundings of my own apartment block, Phuong 19 knows how to take the edge off.

If only someone had told me sooner. I'd been barrelling past the narrow access road that led into this neighbourhood for years, convinced an appreciation of life in Ho Chi Minh City would more likely be established in its historic heart ('Old Saigon'). When I first moved from Hanoi, I brought my old Vespa PX and would sputter across multiple districts just to eat one specific *banh mi* or bowl of noodles on the other side of town.

Why did I feel that I had to pay my respects to the city's most-blogged-about local restaurants anyway? In Hanoi I'd known plenty of expats who supported their adopted hometown with a loyalty you'd expect from die-hard, life-long followers of football clubs.

Migrating south to Saigon, in their eyes, was the ultimate betrayal. Whether saddened or sickened by news of my defection, one Hanoi expat simply emailed an excerpt from a novel by Linh Dinh, a Vietnamese American writer: 'A hodgepodge of incoherence, Saigon thrives on pastiche. Sly, crass, infatuated with all things foreign, it caricatures everyone yet proclaims itself an original.'

This withering, cynical line rankled, but to be honest, I had no riposte. Upon moving south, initially, the gaudier side of the city (the kitsch, the glitz, the rooftop bars and B-list stars) had both caught my eye and baffled me. My food-oriented explorations were, in hindsight, an antidote of sorts, an attempt to eat my way into liking the southern hub. So I rode all over town, seeking out new local dishes – not a bad thing, if your goal is to catalogue as much of the culinary canon as you can. Except with this strategy, I didn't realise what I was missing on my doorstep.

As fate would have it, my long-suffering Vespa eventually stopped working (this time permanently), which encouraged me to explore Phuong 19 on foot.

Traipsing around the area soon became a habit, one which felt different to my crosstown jaunts, because this time, I was chowing down with the locals as a local. I would soon become a regular at places like Luong Ky Mi Gia, an ethnic Chinese family-run restaurant, which serves a mouthwatering bowl of noodles with a braised duck leg, and various Vietnamese descendants of dim sum. Another favourite spot became an eatery called Kaki-Noki, where a chef from Osaka makes Italian and Spanish dishes with Japanese ingredients. There's also a lively beer place that's adjacent to a small park, where I can happily kill the night with pals, sipping icy beers, snacking on tofu in salted egg, skewered prawns, scallops, clams, periwinkles and every other shelled morsel known to man.

To reach these restaurants from my apartment, I often walk down Ngo Tat To Street, where there's a small Catholic church with a modernist design right opposite a pagoda with a statue of Quan Am (the Bodhisattva of Compassion) that faces the adventitious roots of a well-aged banyan tree. All along the roadside, the less religiously inclined also congregate – down from the apartment blocks, and out from the stuffy back alleys, locals of all ages gather in clusters in search of cooler air and communion every evening. Some might be having a quiet tete-a-tete at an outdoor cafe, others might be having a knees-up at a restaurant; some will just carry their own plastic pews from home and plonk themselves down on the pavement and chit-chat with whomever is around.

But everyone, wherever they choose to sit in Phuong 19, tends to face the street in all its captivating glory. Who could blame them? Tellingly, there's a prefix (*con*) for all living things in the Vietnamese language. For example, a cat is *con meo* and a dog is *con cho*. I have always been struck that the word for road is *con duong* – in other words, they're living, breathing things, so when you walk the streets of an old neighbourhood like Phuong 19, you become a part of it.

Later in the evening, I have my own street-watching spot on the two-table terrace of Birdy, a small cocktail bar owned by a friend of mine from Tokyo. Right opposite, there's a local temple with the words *Mieu Ngu Hanh Son* (the Five Elements Temple), which has been built up by nearby residents who come to worship local heroes as tutelary spirits.

It seemed like an appropriate building to be facing some years ago, when Vietnam's national football team bested Malaysia in the final of a regional cup, sparking widespread euphoria throughout the country. Right after the final whistle, crowds of Vietnamese came pouring down the road on motorbikes, waving flags, blaring vuvuzelas, screaming for joy. They were soon followed by foreigners, many clad in Vietnam's colours – football jerseys, headbands, even face paint – who emerged, somewhat tipsily, from various bars and cafes, eager to get into the mix, alive to the possibility of it all. And why not. It's their 'hood, too.

Lost in the back streets

'The flâneur moves through the city with neither a map nor a plan.'

Federico Castigliano

The year I turned forty, a reunified Vietnam reached the same age. I had no lavish plans for my own birthday but Ho Chi Minh City was always going to put on a show for the fortieth anniversary of national reunification. Unsure what I should do or where I should go, I had considered walking around the city to take some photos throughout the day, but April, the hottest of months, coincides with the tail end of the dry season. Post-noon temperatures can hit, and sometimes pass, forty degrees Celisus – not ideal for someone who is genetically engineered to ramble across frosty peat bogs in the depths of Irish winters.

So I decided to bide my time in the hope the city would deliver a signature temperature drop, as it so often does, about an hour before sundown. For many locals that's the moment to escape the office, or stop whatever it is they are doing, and commence street-side socialisation. On wider streets, the early-evening atmosphere can appear fairly rowdy as large groups of office workers or friends gather to raise a glass as one. But I know plenty of folk who prefer to avoid the more rambunctious crowds. Take Chung Hoang Chuong, a former professor at the City College of San Francisco, who left Saigon in the 1960s. Like many *Viet kieu* ('overseas Vietnamese', see glossary), Chuong, a jovial and sociable chap, couldn't resist returning in semi-retirement – the food, the people, the pleasure of chance encounters every time he walks out the door, all part of the allure.

'On the pavement, down a *hem*, or in some cosy cafe, many Saigonese love to find a quiet corner and *chem gio* ('shoot the breeze'),' he told me one day as we cooled off with iced coffees on the third floor of an old apartment block. 'Today, this city is bulging at the seams, but here and there you can see an easy-going essence has endured. I still love to walk around, chit-chat with whoever I meet, and capture that feeling.'

I had no reason to doubt him but I also expected that the reunification party wouldn't be a night for a quiet chat. I was anticipating mass euphoria, a fitting celebration of Ho Chi Minh City and Vietnam's near miraculous growth story. To think that, just over four years after reunification, a fellow by the name of Gabriel García Márquez came to town (on assignment for *Rolling Stone)* and found 'an enormous city, lively and dangerous, with almost four million inhabitants, who go about the streets at all hours because they have nothing else to do.' The CIA and US military used to refer to the American-Vietnam war as 'the show' in conversation but Marquez grimly concluded that the American occupation of Saigon had 'created an artificial paradise, and the cost of this delirium was stupefying.' The city, from what he observed, was filled with widows, orphans, amputees, drug addicts, unemployed bar girls and tuberculars. Pills for seasickness were being sold at a premium to those who planned to steal away in the dead of night on a boat (without really knowing where the boat was going).

Who back then could have imagined the festive mood for the fortieth anniversary, let alone the rising cityscape? From my own neighbourhood, a few kilometres to the east of downtown, I could see one of the newest skyscrapers displaying the national flag with a whole lotta LED – the first signal that everyone should get ready to paint the town red in Vietnam's honour. So, as a woozy, pinkish dusk thickened over the Saigon River, I left my apartment block and jumped into a taxi but ... I wouldn't get far. With a number of high-profile galas and military parades being held, and scores of global media parachuting into town, many central roads were closed to traffic. From the corner of the Saigon Zoo and Botanical Gardens, I had to continue on foot, hoofing it into Little Japan, the unofficial name for a lively warren of streets and alleys peppered with izakaya, yakitori, ramen joints and sake bars.

Ignoring the coos of female staff working at the area's less family-friendly venues, I marched into the heart of Saigon – it's here that various French colonial administrations attempted to transform a swampy frontier town into the ideal metropole through the late nineteenth and early twentieth century. Their urbanism project created tree-lined boulevards, pavements and parks, not to mention stately villas and replicas of the grandest architecture back in the French Third Republic. That, in a nutshell, is how Saigon of Cochinchina came to be branded as the 'Paris of the East', and the 'Pearl of the Orient'. But over the last fifteen years, a growing number of high-rises and skyscrapers have been steadily usurping century-old French colonial structures as the city's most prominent (and photographed) landmarks. Architecturally speaking, you could say Ho Chi Minh City now looks to the east for inspiration with a skyline that has a touch of Shanghai, Seoul and Singapore about it. On the night of the anniversary, I was told Bitexco Financial Tower, the 258-metre-tall summit of the downtown area would be at the centre of the festivities with fireworks being set off on the fifty-second floor helipad.

Still unsure of where I was going to end up later that night, I first wolfed down a bowl of wontons and egg noodles and then headed for a three-star hotel's rooftop bar on Dong Khoi Street, Rue Catinat in French times, where I wanted to pay my respects to the self-titled 'Old Hacks Group,' a bunch of retired and veteran journalists, all of whom had covered the American-Vietnam war at one stage or another, and were having a reunion. At some point in the evening, I sat across from the late photojournalist Tim Page, who was sipping a Saigon Special, puffing on a rollie, and gazing out at the bright lights of a big, brash city he hardly recognised. The Saigon of his yesteryear was, he declared, long gone and it was crystal clear he couldn't wait to leave. But sitting on the rooftop bar, gazing out at the glitzy high-rises, I thought again about what Chuong had said – that a certain spirit endured – and I wondered if it really comes down to us, as individuals, to seek it out ...

In *Sidewalk City*, a book that champions the backstreets of Saigon over its landmarks, the author Annette Kim wrote that she was often unable to point out to friends what was so wonderful about

Ho Chi Minh City from a map. Yet, 'each time I land in the city,' she continued, 'I invariably look for what is different because it has undergone tremendous change. Still, I am usually pleasantly surprised to find how much of the city's charms has remained.'

On the night of the fortieth anniversary, I eventually returned to the streets, where I wandered aimlessly and somewhat against the grain. Hordes of flag-waving locals (most of whom were born long after the country was reunified) were now pouring down District 1's most central thoroughfares in anticipation of the fireworks to come. But I wasn't too fussed about the pyrotechnics; and, feeling a little claustrophobic among the crowds, I strolled up Ham Nghi Street and ducked into a classic Saigon alleyway, where I found what I hadn't known I was looking for – a cluster of tipsy residents-slash-revellers, sitting right outside their homes, some with their tops off, all drinking beers on ice, snacking on various morsels, and, yes, shooting the breeze ...

After I explained that the streets were too hectic for my tastes, they ushered me into the circle and someone handed me a can of beer and a glass of ice. We spent the next hour, going back and forth between languages, speaking of Saigon, and Ho Chi Minh City, the old days, the new days, how they'd never been to the Observation Deck in Bitexco Tower, let alone sat inside the Saigon Opera House. At some stage the fireworks display began but no one budged. We just clinked our glasses together and continued drinking the night away.

*

'Saigonese tend to be more comfortable in unassuming places, that's why there are more stories to be found in the side streets and back alleys,' Dang Duong, a good friend of mine, would tell me later. From her third floor 'HQ,' the Old Compass Cafe, located on Pasteur Street, Duong leads a short walking tour around District 1. But she often strolls around the city simply for her own pleasure, observing the constant changes, and stopping not only to appreciate what remains, but also whatever has suddenly appeared. She walks because it continually restores a feeling of connection with her surroundings. Indeed, in a city that can often feel like it's changing too fast for our liking, walking in Ho Chi Minh City is one way we can slow things down a little and savour the moment. It might sound like a paradox, but a short walk can make one both nostalgic for the city's past and excited about its future.

Of course, with its heavy traffic, pavements that seem more dedicated to the parking of motorbikes, and energy-sapping heat, Ho Chi Minh City could never be described as pedestrian-friendly. The author David Sedaris – an evangelist for the virtues of walking in cities – once described Ho Chi Minh City as the second-worst city for walking he'd ever experienced (Bangkok being the worst). As he was too scared to cross the street, he circled the same block repeatedly, shooing away constant offers for 'massage, sir.' I would bet a small pile of Vietnamese dong that he was walking up Dong Khoi Street and down Nguyen Hue Boulevard, wilting in the heat and counting down the hours until he left. But he's definitely not the only one who has struggled when strolling around downtown. When in the Dong Khoi–Nguyen Hue area, I often see tourists braving the midday sun but looking hot, sweaty and confused, as if they're wondering why they're not sipping cocktails at a beach resort, or snoozing to the sound of lapping waves. On occasion, I have contemplated how these tourists might be encouraged to wander around, fairly aimlessly, and willingly lose their bearings in a city which will always reward the curious-minded wanderer. The American philosopher William James once wrote that our own inner lives are 'fluid, restless, mercurial and always in transition,' which could double as a pretty solid description of Ho Chi Minh City. And perhaps *that's* why it is actually a great place for the walker. Like many of us, the city is a work in progress. A jumble of nerves. A fitful, sometimes impatient place but one that provides an abundance of stimuli which, for some, proves endlessly satisfying.

In *Sidewalk City*, Kim argues that many tourists are

fascinated by everything they see on the city's streets. Furthermore, the spontaneous interactions they have with locals (especially street vendors or other customers enjoying street-side food or drinks) are often a tourist's favourite experience when staying in the city. To help the more fearful of visitors join the fun, she made an interesting proposal – an actual line printed or painted on the pavement. There would be one 3.8-kilometre line in 'Old Saigon,' and another 2.2-kilometre line in Cholon that tourists could follow, nose to the ground, so to speak. It would lead them past local eateries and hidden cultural points of interest, guide them into spaces where they could interact with locals. She even pitched it to the city's Department of Planning and Architecture, who were receptive to the idea and invited her to return with more departments (and tourism experts) at the table.

The project never came to pass, but I always thought it was a fun idea. Tourists would have been able to ditch the paper maps, or avoid staring into their phone, and simply walk along the line and take it all in. Nowadays, there are open-top buses and electric carts that loop around the city's landmarks, which have proven popular, allowing tourists to survey the sights from a cool and breezy vantage point. But I'd still encourage visitors to set aside an hour or three to wander the sidestreets and alleyways. Just not at midday. Or even 2pm. It's best to wait till the afternoon heat begins to recede. And there's no need to walk as if you have a point to prove. Fear not, you'll easily do ten thousand steps. And in this heat? Every step surely counts for double. My advice is to pick a cafe or restaurant as a starting point and then, just wander, freely and slowly. Tan Dinh or Nguyen Thai Binh wards on the edge of District 1 would be my leading suggestions for beginners. But I'm not here to give you a map or an itinerary. I'm only here to tell you that no matter where you go, there will be plenty of sights and curiosities to catch your eye, and as always in Saigon, endless choices to fill your stomach, and countless cafes where you can cool off and recharge.

*

When I last met Chuong to shoot the breeze, he also expressed a wish that visitors could have first-hand encounters with Saigonese hospitality, while revealing his weariness for the outside world's enduring obsession with the American-Vietnam war, which ended more than fifty years ago: 'I'd rather visitors experienced the side-streets and Saigon's alleyway culture than go to the War Remnants Museum or drive to the Cu Chi Tunnels to shoot an AK-47. And thankfully it's still the easiest thing in the world to walk down an alleyway and interact with locals.'

And perhaps this slow, somewhat spontaneous approach has always been the best way to explore

Saigon. Arriving in January, seventy-five years ago, the British travel writer Norman Lewis was underwhelmed by the so-called Paris of the East – might as well call Kingston the 'Oxford of the West Indies,' he sniffed, before noting that 'twenty thousand Europeans keep as much as possible to themselves in a few tamarind-shaded central streets.' With no interest in the city's original expat bubble, or its colonial landmarks, Lewis declared himself disappointed by central Saigon's 'westernised welcome.' But all was not lost. He wilfully plunged into the side streets, and from there, wandered aimlessly, marvelling at a rich tapestry of colourful and puzzling street scenes, including dentists, herbalists, card games, a funeral and a multitude of vendors flogging various foods. After a fruitful perambulation, Lewis must surely have been starting to perspire when he retreated to a local cafe, where he sipped on a bottle of Larue beer as the other customers listened 'respectfully' to 'When Irish Eyes are Smiling' on the radio. This to my mind, three-quarters of a century later, sounds like a quintessential and timeless Saigon moment, one that can only be enjoyed if you set off on foot, without a map, or even a plan.

Cyclogeography
lessons

'Get a bicycle. You will not regret it, if you live.'
Mark Twain, *Taming the Bicycle*

Saigon, 1949.
Deep within an inner-city ward, a young boy sits idly in a doorway among a skein of alleyways, wishing he had someone to play with. But it's after midday, a time when it feels like the whole city has slid into a post-meridian slumber. So the boy wanders down the laneway, kicking the dust up with his feet, only to hear the tintinnabulation of a ding-a-ling bell and, when he looks up, he sees his father wearing a wide grin and riding high on a fetching French bicycle ...

'Oh dad, did you buy a bicycle?! Is it really ours?'

His father gracefully slows to a halt while lifting his right leg over the frame. Then with one hand he pats the saddle to demonstrate his ownership. When neighbours – stirred by the boy's giddy peals of delight – appear in their respective doorways, they each take turns congratulating the boy's father, who has saved up for months to purchase this splendid steed.

For a few weeks, the boy doesn't dare to even ask if he can sit in the saddle, let alone take a spin, although he knows how to ride a bike. But one day, when his father comes home to eat lunch and take a nap, the boy can't resist. He wheels the bicycle out into the alley. The frame is too high for him, but this is not his first rodeo. With one big push on a pedal, suddenly he's up above the frame and in motion. And then? Without originally intending to do so, he exits his alleyway and enters a city that now seems wide open. The boy knows his father will be furious if he finds out about this escapade, but for a few minutes, the boy dares himself not to care. He cycles through the sunshine and into the shade beneath the long slender trees; he feels a breeze blowing through his floppy hair – at one stage he even manages to overtake a horse-drawn carriage – and as he hurries home, hoping to get there before anyone notices he's gone, the boy can't imagine that anyone has ever been this happy ...

*

It's hard to fathom for anyone that has only known Ho Chi Minh City in the twenty-first century, but Saigon used to be defined by its cyclists. In the 1930s there was even a sign that read: *'Piste reservee pour cyclistes'* where Rue Nancy (present day Nguyen Van Cu) met Rue Gallieni (present day Tran Hung Dao).

I know this thanks to Pham Cong Luan, who has written over a dozen books about his hometown. In recent years, Luan has been my go-to whenever I have been delving into the city's history. It's thanks to him I know that, in the late 1940s, owning a splendid bicycle was each Saigonese kid's dream, and that the 1950s were the heyday of the bike in Saigon, a time when every household, rich or poor, owned at least one set of wheels – the most prized bicycles were French brands like Reynolds, Royal Stella, and Peugeot. Just picture the beauty of the morning commute, when the sunlight in Saigon is soft and vague, as a *peloton* of civil servants, university students and high school pupils pedal and glide down one tree-lined street after another. Adding to the elegance of this imagined scene, for those wearing an *ao dai* (a long silk dress), there was a bicycle with a special design – a colourful knitted mesh that covered half of the rear wheel – so their silken tails didn't get caught up in the spokes. And at night? With a dynamo, or two, attached to their bikes, the cyclists collectively lit up the roads as they each wound their way home. For those who had a little leisure time on their hands, owning a bicycle, for the first time in their lives, enabled them to take the long way home, or traverse the town on a whim, visiting neighbourhoods where they didn't live or work, allowing them to feel the pleasure of cycling simply for the sake of cycling and introducing them to the joy of spontaneous urban exploration.

So, what happened? Basically, through the mid-sixties the US military and CIA rolled more and more vehicles into town. Of course, the French had brought in a fair few cars and introduced buses, as well as an automated biped (the iconic Velo Solex), but the Americans fast-tracked Saigon's transformation from a mellow tropical garden city into a smoggy, motorised town. Although, it wasn't just white men in sport shirts and drip-dry pants behind the wheel. 'The American soldier, bumping along in a jeep or a military truck, resents seeing all those Asiatics at the wheels of new Cadillacs,' the journalist and author Mary McCarthy observed, along with billboards advertising Triumphs, Thunderbirds, MGs, Corvettes ('For Delivery Here or Stateside, Payment on Easy Terms').

Surveying the scene after getting stuck in a traffic jam, and trying to get over the culture shock she felt from being in what looked like 'a stewing Los Angeles, shading into Hollywood, Venice Beach, and Watts,' McCarthy, like so many of us have done in Saigon, couldn't help feeling a sense of loss for a former version of the city, one that she had never seen with her own eyes: 'Even removing the sandbags and the machine guns, and restoring the trees that have been chopped down to widen the road to the airport, the mind cannot excavate what Saigon must have been like "before".'

But when the price of gasoline began to rise in the early seventies, the bicycle would once again become a leading mode of transport for adults and, especially, students. As a result of Saigon's changing economic fortunes, the bicycle would continue to be a common mode of transport for many through the late seventies and the eighties. Many friends who visited or came to live in the early nineties, recall bicycles being far more prominent on the streets. However, by then every household dreamed of having a motorbike (or two), just as nowadays many dream of having a car (or two) in what is one of the most revved-up cities in the world. Statistics vary, but a couple of years ago it was reported that Ho Chi Minh City had 8.8 million registered vehicles, including nearly 900,000 cars – for a population of ten million. As more vehicles continually drive in and out of the city from other provinces, we can assume that on any given day, there could be over a million cars and over nine million motorbikes clogging the streets.

Some might think: who would want to cycle in such a city? I do, for one, although it took me a while to even think of buying a bike. When I first migrated to Ho Chi Minh City, nearly thirteen years ago, I never noticed anyone cycling for the fun of it. Every cyclist I saw had a purpose or cycled out of economic necessity. Pupils pedalling home from school; home-cooks bound for the nearest wet market; bicycle-based vendors selling *banh mi*, flowers from the Central Highlands, or seasonal fruits from the Mekong Delta, and the odd hardworking scrap picker. At lunchtime, I spotted more than one dextrous fellow balancing bowls of noodle soup on a tray over his head while steering his bicycle with one hand (a very local style of delivery service). And when I was hanging out anywhere near the backpacker area, sometimes I'd see (and hear) a cycling masseur roving the streets while jangling a set of keys to attract customers.

As my network expanded, I did meet some expats with bicycles, but they weren't casual cyclists, they were MAMILs (middle-aged men in lycra), who jumped into the saddle more to escape, not explore, the city. Of course, there were others taking more leisurely spins around town. It's just that I was blind to them until a global pandemic came along. For a period we were all free to roam in Ho Chi Minh City, but there wasn't really anywhere to go (gyms, cinemas, clubs, etc., were all shuttered; cafes and restaurants were reduced to doing deliveries only). So I bought a seven-speed Townie, which in a city without a single hill is all you require. I also got some lights and a helmet, but no lycra. As the musician David Byrne, a keen urban cyclist, remarks in his *Bicycle Diaries*: 'You don't really need the spandex.' Then, every evening, I took to pedalling around in no particular direction, taking great pleasure from being able to alleviate my cabin fever. I was happy to burn a few calories along the way, but the effect on my mental health far outweighed the physical benefits, and I soon started to wonder why I hadn't thought of buying a bike before.

I wasn't the only one trying to cycle my way out of the lockdown blues. Bicycle sales in Ho Chi Minh City surged at this time. And with far fewer automated vehicles around (no buses, no trucks, no taxis, etc.), everyone who roamed around got a glimpse at what being bike-friendly can do for a city. Every time I cycled alongside the Nhieu Loc–Thi Nghe Canal, a breezy nine-kilometre waterway that snakes across the city, I saw cyclists, solo and in clusters, who, like me, were making the most of the relatively light traffic. During the pandemic years, the city also got its first bike sharing scheme (TNGO), which was quickly trending on Tiktok and Instagram. Cycling, all of sudden, became a thing. For a little while anyway.

When the motorised traffic returned to full

throttle, I continued to cycle across town, two or three times a week, although my routes and habits had to change. No more freewheeling down Dong Khoi Street to the Saigon River, or circling a desolate Ben Thanh Market. It's impossible to avoid major streets on any crosstown cycle, but you never have to go far before there's an opportunity to slip into a side road, backstreet or, best of all, an alleyway where the four-wheelers can't follow. And on pretty much every aimless exploration, just like when I walk with no destination in mind, I usually find *something* – a beautiful (or spooky) modernist building, a street food joint that seems to be calling my name out, a super-mellow backstreet, a wet market, a rickety bridge ...

Sometimes I'll pedal all the way to Cholon, home to pagodas, temples, apothecaries, iconic apartment blocks, a million small businesses and a gazillion restaurants. Sometimes I'll breeze around leafier parts of town, like Da Kao Ward and District 3, where you can still find sumptuous art deco villas and stylish modernist buildings. And sometimes, I'll head all the way to Thanh Da, a curious peninsula and urban area with a countryside vibe, or spin alongside the train tracks that run through Phu Nhuan, one of the knottier districts, where I occasionally have to peek at Google Maps to see where the hell I am.

But mostly I enjoy just whirring through the city and absorbing its rhythms, furtively observing everything I pass. On occasion, I might think about a story that I'm working on, and if I am really lucky, the ending to a story like this one starts to materialise (or at least seem within reach). Quite often I don't think about anything in particular. I just cycle for the sake of cycling, to capture that feeling of stillness in motion that only an urban cyclist can experience, and to embrace the sense of calm that I now know is possible amid the motorised chaos.

Falling for old Saigon

'The past is a foreign country; they do things differently there.'

L.P. Hartley

Nearly a decade ago, Ho Chi Minh City's most central *bia hoi* joint ('fresh beer,' see glossary) bit the dust. On this drinking institution's final evening, a smattering of expatriates – viewing this closure as regrettable, poignant, even symbolic – stopped by to toast the end of an era alongside the garrulous and gentlemanly bowsies that frequented the place, which was housed in an old modernist building on a plot of land earmarked for redevelopment.

Two or three years later, a similar scene played

out in another downtown drinking den called Hien & Bob's. After president Bill Clinton ordered the lifting of the US trade embargo on Vietnam, back in the mid-nineties, Hien & Bob's dusty Tiki bar comforted homesick American businessmen with 'real ham and cheese sandwiches' and, of course, cold beer served by attractive young women. The Americans were back and so too were the bar girls.

Although Bob – an American war veteran who had returned to Vietnam as a civilian in the early nineties – shuffled off this mortal coil a long time ago, Hien, a frosty host well-known for her icy burns, kept it going (even the ham and cheese sandwiches). But for as long as I lived in the city, business never seemed brisk. It felt like what it was – a bar from another era. Nonetheless, like the *bia hoi* joint, Hien & Bob's still had a place in people's hearts, perhaps because it was a throwback venue in a rapidly modernising town. Even people who never went there didn't want it to close. It was, for many of us, a comforting fixture. A piece of the urban tapestry we often passed and didn't want to see peeled away.

On the night Hien would be serving her last icy cold Tiger beer, a horde of expat revellers kindly gathered to bid her a fond farewell. With some artistic licence furnishing my memories, I now picture Hien and a dozen punters, all linking arms behind the bar, and singing this town's favourite Mary Hopkins song, that classic ode to the good old days, the one that begins: 'Once upon a time, there was a tavern, where we used to raise a glass or two ...'

*

When each of these two old watering holes shut their doors, I was struck by two strands of nostalgia intertwining in the minds of some expats. The first was about harking back to the good old days – *their* good old days i.e. that time when they were younger, carefree, and rarely regretted drinking for six hours, for no particular reason, on a Tuesday night. It was a time when Saigon was much less 'hipsterised.' No IPAs with flowery adjuncts. No pretentious smoke-infused potations. No specialty coffee joints with fully washed Nicaraguan beans. The street-side beer joints, dingy bars and old school cafes were all they needed to get their fix and make an emotional connection with the city that buzzed and crackled all around them. Those who attended the farewells no longer drank regularly at Hien & Bob's or the *bia hoi* – and perhaps they never had – but the loss of these old-school institutions reminded them of who they were when they first arrived and swiftly fell in love with the city.

This kind of reaction to the city's rapid transformation is far from unusual. You could even argue it's timeless. Back in mid-sixties, the Associated Press's Saigon bureau chief, Edwin Q White, penned an article lamenting the rate of change, traffic issues and noise pollution, and mocking those who still branded the city the 'Paris of the East.' 'The Saigon that perhaps never was, certainly is no more.' White had arrived only two years earlier, and yet there he was, pining for the good old days, *his* good old days.

The second strand of nostalgia I have noted is perhaps more complex, but here's an attempt to simplify it. There are many long-term residents who are simultaneously infatuated by the postcard-aesthetics of 'Old Saigon' and disillusioned with the digital renderings of 'twenty-first century Ho Chi Minh City.' The former is romantic, storied and characterful. The latter is glitzy but generic, svelte but soulless. It's the 'Tomorrowland' that they didn't sign up for and don't want to wake up in. More distressingly, as it grows, it threatens the physical spaces where they forged so many happy memories.

Nostalgia is a skilled revisionist. It can even make us pine for a period of history when we weren't alive. One evening at a small cocktail bar in a rapidly gentrifying part of Binh Thanh District, another customer pulled out a grainy picture of his grandfather as a dapper young man on the streets of Saigon in the 1930s. In the background there were vintage cars, the Saigon Opera House and the Hotel Continental, all frozen in time. 'Wow! Those really were the days ...' someone gushed, seeing everything literally and figuratively in black and white, perhaps imagining only the pleasures of a congestion-free colonial town, like sipping vermouth cassis on a terrace, or trading glances with well-heeled beauties while ambling down Rue Catinat, the colonial town's most fashionable street, and obviously *not* thinking of the day-to-day realities for, say, a malnourished rickshaw rider, a peasant labourer, a prostitute, an incarcerated revolutionary, a mother of five whose husband is fated to die fighting his own brethren, or someone stricken with dysentery, syphilis, typhoid, opiomania ...

Whatever quaint and idyllic atmosphere that person was picturing, they rejoined: 'Man, it must have been beautiful back then.' Because nostalgia colours everything rosily and shears the past of complexity, whether it's the past we never experienced, or our own 'good old days.' In a giant work of progress like Ho Chi Minh City, where the dust never settles, it often feels like the past is increasingly being idealised. Is that because of how fast the present is vanishing? All over the city you'll see vintage signs above fashion stores or noodle chains, hear vinyl recordings in retro-styled bars. On a recent wander from District 1 to District 3, I even discovered a cafe in a newly built building that had been painstakingly decorated in an authentic modernist style. Its target market? Fashionable locals under twenty-five.

What would any of these kids, or indeed any

of us, make of the place, if we were whisked back to, say, the early seventies through a spiralling time machine? Frank Snepp, former CIA analyst and author of *Decent Interval*, described Saigon at that time as a 'grimy imitation of Dodge City' where cashed-up, horny GIs had the run of the place, eating burgers made of water buffalo meat at girly bars. Locals had, he noted, either withdrawn or were cooking up schemes to profit. Shabbiness clung to the city like a scab. Oh, and it reeked of urine.

When an establishment they once frequented closes, certainly many long-term expats are prone to seeing its loss as symbolic. But how we view change in the city is often shaped by our own self-centred narratives, and people tend to overlook how they, and their starry notions, have changed along the way, too. Can an expat be genuine when lamenting the closure of an 'age-old' family run eatery or old-school bar in District 1, if they now spend their days and nights in a suburban expat bubble like Thao Dien, a place where expats quickly forget why they even came to Vietnam, mainly because they're too busy arguing about who now makes the best tacos, or where they should go for a boozy brunch on Sunday?

Admittedly, in central Ho Chi Minh City, when a business like Hien & Bob's closes, there's often a secondary concern – the building. After Hien's last call, many would have assumed the whole building – an old apartment block, utterly dilapidated – would soon be levelled. Like many aged structures in Saigon, it could look somewhat charming on a sunny day, or when a seductive twilight snuggled around it. But on a drab, late-rainy-season afternoon, when I pointed it out to a pair of visitors, adding that it might soon be a thing of the past, one responded flatly: 'Well, no great loss.' The other visitor suggested, diplomatically, that in Tokyo it would have been demolished decades ago but in Helsinki, they'd insist on keeping it. Walking toward the Saigon River that day, I got a closer look at the building and realised that it was little more than a shell. None of the upper floors appeared to be occupied. Most of the ground floor shops weren't just shuttered. They were gutted. The only sign of life came from a shop selling Cuban cigars and top-shelf liquors where Hien had once plied her trade. Like her bar, I realised, the building had run its race.

One building that did get razed, more than a decade ago now, was the Tax Centre on the corner of Nguyen Hue and Le Loi boulevards. If you were to look at a picture of the building in its pomp, when it was called Les Grands Magasins Charner, and everything was sepia-toned, serene and seductive, you might be aghast. However, if you were to see the building in its last days, when its facade had lost all of its original charm, you might also think, as I did,

'Well, no great loss ...' although inside the building there was a staircase – created using the Moroccan mosaic art of zellij – worth saving. According to local news reports, this piece of heritage was carefully removed and stored so it could be resurrected one day, perhaps embedded in whatever eventually gets built on the site, which remains vacant. Judging by social media, some viewed the demolition of the Tax Centre as scandalous, and many were sceptical the staircase would be seen again. But it's worth stressing that, as a retail space, it was no longer a place of purpose. Modern malls elsewhere had usurped all of the mini-fashion outlets upstairs. Perhaps the jewellers downstairs ticked over but they never seemed too busy whenever I stuck my head in (to get a blast of aircon, not to buy anything). Every city eventually sheds the businesses and removes the buildings it doesn't need. And so it goes.

But 'Old Saigon'? I believe its spirit is still here, even if its form continues to change more quickly than a human heart can bear. I have learned that whatever it is you truly love about this city, you have to keep going to it and savouring it. In doing so, you keep breathing life into the old spaces and places you cherish. And if by chance you see me down the tavern, the one where we used to raise a glass or two, and laughed away the hours, let's smile at one another and sing: 'Those were the days, my friend, we thought they'd never end ...'

CHECK
OUT

Sent in hope

If there's one grand old building in Ho Chi Minh City that I was guilty of taking for granted, for many years, it was the Saigon Central Post Office. Constructed between 1886 and 1891, it is one of the city's most famous landmarks from the French colonial period. Whenever I passed by the building, I mostly noted tourists in conical hats and locals posing for photo shoots, and pressed on.

But one day, a short writing assignment that came my way forced me to give the building a little more thought. In search of a quote, I contacted my trusty local source, Pham Cong Luan, who enlightened me on the Central Post Office's significance to his generation. 'It was for many of us a place to write and send letters in hope.' These missives he speaks of were sent to dear friends who had taken their chances and moved overseas in the late seventies and early eighties, before the US finally lifted its embargo in the mid-nineties, and when impoverished Vietnam was still isolated from much of the world. Luan and his overseas friends wouldn't have known when they would cross paths again.

After chatting with Luan, I decided to visit the Central Post Office. It was a Tuesday afternoon. A skin-scorching sunny spell had finally relented and a late rainy season shower loomed. Stepping into the building's cooler air, I took the opportunity to write a quick postcard to one of my late mother's best friends in Dublin. She's getting on, as they say, and Luan's talk of 'sending a letter in hope' echoed in my mind as I dropped the card on top of a basket filled with envelopes and postcards. In Saigon, rather sweetly in this digital age, sending 'snail mail' is a throwback-thing-to-do for tourists, but many Vietnamese still come here to avail themselves of postal services, too. There's another location around the corner on Nguyen Du Street – the 'actual post office' as a friend of mine likes to call it. But given the choice, a fair few locals clearly still choose the showpiece venue. Perhaps it adds an extra lick of luck to a college application also sent in hope.

As I did a lap of the interior under the high arched ceiling, a small number of Vietnamese were sitting on benches by wooden tables, busily filling out applications, or taking care of bills, seemingly oblivious to the throng of tourists (domestic and foreign) taking pictures and queuing for stamps. It's on those benches where Luan would have sat, all those years ago when Saigon was, in so many places, a downtrodden town. I stopped and tried to picture him there: a handsome, bespectacled fellow in his early twenties, wearing a short-sleeved shirt over a vest tucked into his trousers. Like all scribes, he is armed with his tools – one pen in a shirt pocket, another in his hand. He writes multiple letters, releasing so many emotions that he begins to feel lightheaded. As he writes out a foreign address on an envelope, he cannot really picture the city where a friend lives. He can only imagine it hazily and wonder what life must be like there for his friends. He then buys some stamps from someone behind the counter and, with a quiet act of ceremony, he places his letters on a heaped pile of envelopes, hoping that each one will find its way into the hands of the intended recipient. With the business of correspondence concluded, he steps out into the late afternoon sun, which in Saigon often feels softer, kinder, more forgiving. While Luan was lost in the act of letter writing, a downpour has been and gone. He hadn't even noticed the deluge from inside the Central Post Office. A whiff of petrichor hangs in the air. The streets glisten. The trees look more lush, Notre Dame Cathedral more pink. Everything is so vivid that he half wonders if he has stepped into a dream. He takes a few tentative steps and then turns to look back at the building he has just exited. In the golden sunlight, he sees the intricate details of the century-old facade more clearly than ever. A line of verse springs to mind: *'Thanh pho dep nhu trang hoang tro lai'* ('The city is beautiful once again'). Then he walks away, not just hoping but *believing* that one day he and his friends will meet again, maybe even here in this city, the one he knows they still love. The one they carry in their hearts. The one they will forever call home.

How to love a rainy season

To love the rainy season in Saigon, for starters you must be well-sheltered, and preferably snug. A rule of thumb: the more happily ensconced you are, the more you will enjoy the sight and sound of the heavens opening. Let the clouds burst, you will think, as I have everything I need right here.

Not only must you be perfectly content with your surroundings, but nobody can be waiting for you on the other side of town. You must have nowhere to go, no errands to run, no meetings to attend, or people to chase. You should be free to procrastinate.

Yes, it would be advantageous to live in an area where the flooding of streets is minimal (not just for your sake but also for the guy delivering your pizza – don't forget to tip him generously). If you are at home, do what you like as you sit out a rainstorm. Fall asleep reading a book. Think of a great opening line to a poem you'll never write. Strum something with strings. Make the mother of all sandwiches. Send a certain someone a text that makes their day. Picture the pleasure of leaving your apartment later on, when the weather is cool and the air is fresh.

There will, of course, be days and times throughout the rainy season where you will have to leave your place of shelter knowing that rain is imminent. It is helpful, therefore, to have a wide view of the skyline so you can watch the clouds roll in, and roll away again (it's also beneficial to have a friend, who has a view of the other side of the city, and responds quickly to text messages).

When you need to leave home, do so with plenty of time to spare. There might not be statistics to support this claim, but the most dangerous time to ride a motorbike in Saigon is undoubtedly the ten-minute period just before a rainstorm, when legions of motorcyclists tend to 'ride it like they stole it' – and oddly, many car drivers seemingly also feel the urge to accelerate through traffic and slalom their way to shelter.

Whenever you leave your abode, bring a bag. In that bag have all your preferred tools for whiling away time: a book, a Kindle, or a magazine; a notepad or sketchbook and pens; and most importantly, rechargers for all your gadgets.

Should you be in a cafe alone, it's still nice to have a sense of company. A smattering of other customers, preferably ones who seem both intriguing and/or attractive to you. They are strangers, but for the duration of the rainstorm, you will sit together, staring out the window, contemplating and daydreaming as one, like fellow travellers on a train hurtling into a familiar heartland. Conversation is optional. Should it occur it will be cordial, if not pleasant, and all participants will instinctively know when it has run its course. Resist the urge to rush home – remember that the rainy season doesn't cause traffic jams; millions of people all trying to flee the city centre at the same time does. Appreciate the sense of cosiness that can be created only by the sound of a deluge outside.

Perhaps, if you're really lucky you might not want to rush because you're face to face with someone you can't get enough of – a lover, or someone you want to be your lover; a great conversationalist, a witty and erudite person; someone who makes you belly laugh and/or see familiar things in a new way; or just someone you want to gaze at admiringly. 'I hope it rains all day,' you might think, or be corny enough to say. And maybe someday that will come to pass.

The Saigonese have a dated expression, 'the sun shines in the morning, the rain falls in the afternoon,' and some old timers will claim to remember a time when it rained for thirty-five minutes every day at precisely two-thirty in the afternoon during the rainy season. Now the rains come and go when they please. They seem to arrive earlier in the year, and linger for longer, too. Last year, the more the rainy season went on, the more tumultuous it became. For much of October, it felt more like a stormy season. These new erratic weather patterns make people who dislike the rainy season only more woebegone with the sight of each and every rainstorm. Their greatest fear? That one of these years there will be a rainy season that never ends. Should you find yourself surrounded by people who complain about rainy days in the rainy season, say nothing. Instead, start drafting a text or an email and confess to a dear old friend: 'If it weren't for all the damage to local businesses, the flooding of streets, the threat of water-borne diseases, and the widespread misery, I'd be more comfortable telling people that I love the rainy season.' Then delete the draft and decide to write a lover's guide to the rainy season instead.

Here's to the afterlife

'Aren't you afraid of ghosts?' I asked.
Over the line, in the silence, the static hissed.
'You aren't afraid of the things you believe in,' he said.
Viet Thanh Nguyen, *The Refugees*

As a lifelong atheist, I'm not just sceptical of the paranormal. Gods and spirits? In my mind they are all a fantasy. You know, like Santa Claus and the Loch Ness monster. So when I told a Saigonese friend I wanted to write a story about the ghosts that supposedly wander the city, she wasn't convinced I was the right man for the job.

'You can visit places that are said to be haunted but you won't feel anything,' she said matter-of-factly, before explaining that only someone who is *yeu bong via* ('light in spirit') can sense when they are in the presence of a ghost.

But could I compensate for my lack of clairvoyance with a little old-school psychogeography? As a hazy sun began to fade, causing the late afternoon shadows to slip away, I decided to take a speculative wander around Le Van Tam Park, which in colonial times was a dedicated cemetery, mainly for Europeans, who a hundred years ago lived in fear of deadly diseases like cholera, bubonic plague, malaria and smallpox. As the graveyard was located at the end of Rue Bangkok (Mac Dinh Chi today), long-term emigres apparently used to joke with ailing accomplices: 'See you on Bangkok Street.' (I came across this historical nugget in *Down and Out in Saigon: Stories of the Poor in a Colonial City* by Haydon Cherry.)

Whatever killed them off, their corpses were collectively disinterred, more than forty years ago now, and today you'll find a large, leafy green space with a soporific vibe and some sturdy socialist sculptures in its place. Whenever I walk through the park in the early afternoon, the heat and humidity have me begging for a breeze; but once the city starts to cool down, the park quickly fills with life – you'll see joggers, hip-hop dancers, matches of ping pong and *da cau* ('foot badminton,' see glossary). Idlers and daydreamers, too.

I once read that ghost stories were commonly told about the park after the mass exhumation in the eighties. That had me picturing a disgruntled French ghoul staggering under the moonlight in search of a *pousse-pousse* (rickshaw) to ferry him down to Grand Cafe de la Terrasse by the Saigon Opera House, or some other colonial haunt, for a much-needed stiff drink. But that fantasy fizzled when my trusty source, Luan, said: 'I am not sure the Saigonese were ever bothered by French ghosts. Why not? Perhaps because they weren't close to them in day-to-day-affairs in this world, so they had no connection with them in the afterlife either.'

Sensing that I should look for a more contemporary ghost story, I recalled the time I bumped into an acquaintance – a physio with sleeve tattoos and Instagrammable good looks. I was sitting in the cafe where I go to write and gaze out at the languid Saigon River. Normally, the physio just grabbed a coffee-to-go, but that day, he sat down inside as he'd been told to steer clear of his apartment for a few hours. His girlfriend – a cosmopolitan yet traditional young woman from Saigon – had apparently heard one too many strange noises late at night. In certain corners, there was cold air – not a good sign. 'She says there's a ghost hanging about, so she's up there doing some sort of exorcism,' he said with a shrug.

It's not unusual for Vietnamese to believe that a ghost might be meddling in someone's love life. The word *duyen am* can be translated as 'a connection with unliberated spirits.' For anyone who is unlucky in love, and remains single, the suspicion of fretting elders is that a spirit from a past life – an old lover or jealous admirer – is clinging on from the other side. They (the single person) are advised to make an offering at a pagoda, so the old flame releases their grip. One female friend, who is unmarried and now forty, told me her parents make annual trips to the pagoda in the hope that they can liberate the spirit that must, surely, be scaring off suitors. Judging by a pop song called '*Duyen Am*,' younger generations have given the word a more whimsical meaning. In the song, the singer Hoang Thuy Linh is trying to shake off an unwanted stalker, someone who is following her around like a tail. The singer mocks the man, offering him sticky rice and chicken – a standard way of warding off a wandering ghost, but I'll get back to that later ...

So, if you're in Saigon and there's something strange in your neighbourhood, who ya' gonna call? In the Violet Kupersmith novel *Build Your House Around My Body*, it's the Saigon Spirit Eradication Co., which could be a pretty solid startup idea (bro, build the app, and they will download it). But in reality, the physio's girlfriend would likely have called a *thay cung* (a monk, but perhaps we should use the word shaman), someone who conducts rituals to communicate with the spirit world, ward off evil spirits, and ensure good fortune for individuals or families. Oh, and businesses, too – ghost busting, or rather ghost *cleansing,* is a lucrative industry. Developers, realtors and banks will even have a budget for dealing with unwanted spirits. For example, if a house that has been abandoned for many years gets repossessed by a bank, they would hire a *thay cung* to cleanse the premises and give life to the 'coffin rooms' within (yes, so they can flog it).

Every newly built real estate project – from major to minor – will also get a *thay cung* to perform an offering to the spirits of the deceased. I was once told that the developer of a large apartment project in Ho Chi Minh City burned a cool 500 million dong (about US$20,000) to spiritually cleanse the land.

But wait, I hear you ask – who are the ghosts that may or not be spotted (or felt) in these houses and construction sites? In Vietnamese culture, wandering ghosts tend to be spirits who have not been formally buried or cremated (often they are said to be soldiers killed in battle). They may have a grievance with whomever killed them or they may simply be stuck between worlds. The key thing to understand is that nobody tries to eradicate or obliterate these wandering ghosts in the style of a Hollywood Ghostbuster, who would suck the spectre up into a 'proton pack' or blast it with a particle thrower (I know, how very American). And there's no need for any kind of grisly exorcism. The

Vietnamese way is all about reconciliation. You appease these sad, angry and hungry (*really, bloody hungry*) spirits with offerings. Chicken, sticky rice, hard liquor, cigarettes, Choco Pies – whatever you think they'd fancy.

A quick but useful story. Once upon a time, there was a boy called Kien Muc Lien who reached enlightenment at an early age. Unfortunately his mother had a more chequered existence and, upon her death, she was sentenced to spend eternity being tormented by demons and ghosts and, even more distressingly, left in constant pain of hunger. Kien Muc Lien wanted to find a way to get food through to her in the hereafter, but he knew the demons would just incinerate whatever he sent. So he turned to Buddha, who told him to hold a special ceremony, which would become known as *vu lan* ('wandering soul'). Basically, when he prayed for his mother's soul and asked for her sins to be forgiven, his offering of food passed through and his famished mum got to eat.

Although this Buddhist legend is Indian in its origin, the Vietnamese people have made it their own and *Le Vu Lan* (Wandering Soul Festival) is now a major religious occasion, celebrated on the fifteenth day of the seventh month of the lunar calendar. During what is called 'ghost month' (the seventh lunar month), the doors to the underworld are opened. It's considered to be a turbulent time in the land of the living. Not wishing to tempt fate with all those hungry ghosts moping around, many locals become risk averse in that month – for example, they won't buy a house, or a car; they won't get married, or sign a business contract.

During the American-Vietnam war, when someone from US military intelligence got wind of the above deep-rooted beliefs, they devised a sly strategy to spook the enemy called 'Operation Wandering Souls.' Recordings of eerie noises, funereal music and wailing ghostly voices were played in the jungle and from helicopters with mounted speakers, in an attempt to freak out the enemy, so they would run away, defect, or perhaps just lose their minds. In one recording called 'Ghost Tape No. 10,' whimpering children call out 'Come Home Daddy!' and disembodied men wail, 'My friends, I come back to let you know that I am dead ... I am dead. I am in hell ... just hell. It was a senseless death. How senseless ...'

Even if the Vietnamese soldiers targeted by this piece of psychological warfare believed there were ghosts in the jungle, I guess they could have just launched a counter operation – an offering of food accompanied by a sincere prayer for the aggrieved spirit to be at peace. Yeah, stick that on a helmet: *Make offerings, not war.*

*

One night while having beers in a refurbed modernist building – that was once abandoned and believed to be haunted – I got talking to a local graffiti artist, a very modern-looking, tattooed guy who admitted that he believed in ghosts. But even if they spooked him out from time to time, he was not afraid to approach them. He told me that every year, he and a posse of pals would head to the countryside and find a house for 'painting.' One year they rode motorbikes to Sa Dec, a town that grew from riparian trade in the Mekong Delta. On its outskirts, the graffiti artists found a shell of an old colonial villa where no one had lived for decades. Respectful young guys and gals that they are – taggers with manners? – they asked around town and found the landlord. Would he allow them to access the ground for a day of painting? 'I don't mind if you go in there but you should know there are ghosts there,' said the landlord. 'Japanese soldiers killed Vietnamese inside there in 1945 and the spirits of those men remain. You must make an offering, if you want to hang out there.' So they did just that.

But ghost-cleansing rituals don't always do the job. In another era, the President Hotel was one of the trendiest accommodations in 'Old Saigon.' It had a rooftop swimming pool, a ballroom hall and 530 apartments, making it large enough to be transformed into the BEQ (Bachelor Enlisted Quarters) for the US military, which rented the whole building in 1964.

The President Hotel was developed by a man called Nguyen Doi Tan, a native of An Giang province, who had become one of the richest men in Saigon. One spurious urban tale claimed that Tan had refused to bypass the number thirteen when doing the interior, which condemned the building to bad luck from the very beginning. Through the eighties and nineties, the building was much neglected, even if people continued to live inside, and slowly slid into a state of disrepair. Infamy then followed. In one ghost story, people on the street kept seeing a lady falling from a height. Locals weren't surprised as a former resident had once jumped from the tenth floor. Those who were at the scene claimed that when they stood over the woman's corpse, her eyes were wide open. When someone tried to close them, and give her peace, they couldn't. Neighbours and bystanders all took turns, but the woman's eyes remained wide open. I have no doubt that within minutes someone was making an offering in a bid to appease her spirit.

Another report I found online quoted a former resident of the building: 'Oh yes, there were many ghosts. They filled the staircases and the corners. Every time I climbed the stairs, I felt chills down my spine as a gust of wind blew at my face. I knew that they were messing with me. From the ground floor to the rooftop, they were everywhere. I guess that the one with a *yeu bong via* had more chances of seeing them.'

By the time a number of foreign photographers came to document (and somewhat glorify) the building it was a dimly lit dump, where minimal income families and squatters dwelled. The walls were alive with mould. The pipes and staircases had turned to rust. In one stairwell, someone had sprayed the word *ma* ('ghost,' see glossary). Its only redeeming feature was being photogenic, so the photographers kept coming. When researching this story, I even found an image that looks like something out of a fashion shoot with a western woman in a flowing gown perched between the exposed rafters. But for those who actually lived in the building, ghosts included, one can only hope they have all moved on to a better place. Nine years ago, the whole dilapidated structure was finally razed. Aware of the ghost stories, the builders and developers set up an altar and, after a half month of offerings, they broke ground. There's no building there today. Just a metal fence that has sealed off the foundations. It's an absence that can trick the heart into missing what was, in reality, a slum.

Another infamous building associated with various ghost stories is Thanh Kieu Plaza in Cholon. It's a colossal mixed-use residential and commercial high-rise complex covering an area of 9,971 square metres with three thirty-three-floor towers that were designed to make the project look like a ship with three chimneys. However, locals felt the structure reminded them of three incense sticks, which in turn only reminds them of the dead. The rent was also too high, and the tiny Hong Kong-style apartments proved unpopular with the local market. It was never a success but over the years incidents and accidents – a blazing fire and a murder-suicide – fuelled rumours that the whole place was cursed. Once considered a symbol of the city's bright future, the building, now over twenty-five years old, is a mostly desolate and eerie-looking structure. Some years ago, a new owner purchased it for over 600 billion dong (about US$25 million). They repainted the facade with a lick of green, rebranded it 'Garden Mall,' and I have no doubt that they burned a helluva lot of incense and made repeated offerings, but the property market didn't bite or even nibble. When I visited, the only signs of life were on the ground floor where a number of Asian F&B franchises were operating. It seemed like a particularly odd place to go for anyone craving Taiwanese buns or Korean hotpot, but there were customers in each restaurant. Even more curiously, I spotted two tourists talking to a guide wearing an *ao dai*. The theme of the city tour they were on? Haunted spaces in Ho Chi Minh City. Pretty creepy, if you ask me.

*

It was only after I visited a few supposedly haunted sites in Ho Chi Minh City that a Saigonese friend pointed out that most ghosts in the city are not wandering around but easily found. You could even count them in a census, if you wanted, because the dead mostly don't move on. They're happily ensconced at home, still communing with their loved ones through the family altar and enjoying the offerings that keep them well-fed and upwardly mobile in the afterlife.

Most Vietnamese feel a great sense of duty to their ancestors. They are, simply by being alive, in debt to the family that has gone before. Some Saigonese friends who are Christians still maintain a family altar in their house (if you're going to be religious, why not hedge your bets?) and follow the tradition of commemorating death anniversaries with a home-cooked meal. This occasion, called *dam gio* (see glossary), is a way for descendants to honour an ancestor. At the *dam gio* I have attended in Saigon, there have been beers (lots of beers) and loads of delicious food, usually whatever the ancestor enjoyed eating the most. A quiet prayer by the altar will be made by each of the descendants but it's never a grave or sombre occasion. It's really all about gathering the clan and breathing life and happiness into the room. Some of the nicest meals I've had in Saigon have been at a family home for a death anniversary, which might sound strange to some, but they are always joyful affairs. Tales are told, jokes are made, glasses are continually raised. And if the spirit really is there, they'd surely be smiling. I am not a religious man, but I feel this is a tradition I can get behind. So if my ancestors wish to host a *dam gio* in my honour, after I shuffle off this mortal coil, they have my blessing. Let there be roasted quail, crab spring rolls, sticky rice, a crunchy chicken salad, Irish black pudding, and cans of Guinness. And Choco Pies.

Tet is oh so quiet

According to the venerable scholar and historian Dr Huu Ngoc, *Tet* (see glossary) in Vietnam is a time for man to commune with nature as well as a time for the living to honour the dead. It is also a time for family reunions and reconciliations and, if you're really filled with the joys of Spring, perhaps a detente with a neighbour (say, one who's been renovating their house for months on end, and really getting on your wick).

If you are Vietnamese, that is.

For non-Vietnamese living in Ho Chi Minh City, ones without ties to local families, it's a different story. *Tet*, if anything, is a time to pack the bags and run for the hills, or more likely a beach destination of choice – Samui, Bali, Langkawi, *wherever-i*.

Relative newcomers to town will be warned of a *Tet*-rifying scenario: everything is shut, there's nowhere to go, nothing to do, and most alarmingly, nobody around to do things for you. Imagine staying put and then your Wi-Fi conks out ... *The horror.*

If anyone is wavering, unsure whether they should stay or go, the build-up to *Tet* is often a supreme deal-breaker. The volume of the *Tet* tunes gets cranked up to eleven. The ungovernable traffic is more feral than ever. Some folks feel the pressure and get a little, well, *tetchy*. Others (already following the moon, burdened by preparations, or planning when and how to return to their ancestral homeland) get distracted. 'Maybe after *Tet*,' becomes a standard reply for all service providers. It all seems to cry out: 'Book a ticket and get out of here.'

For all of the above reasons, it's generally assumed no one would voluntarily stick around when they don't have to. That's why before the holiday actually begins, everyone I meet will typically ask, 'So where are you going for *Tet*?'

When I answer that I'm staying in Ho Chi Minh City, there is usually some confusion. I can see people thinking: 'But ... *why?*'

A couple of years ago, perhaps the thought of staying here and living with limited services, gave some folk too many flashbacks of Covid-19 lockdowns. But, of course, we're free to roam far and wide during *Tet*, and the further and wider you roam, the more you'll appreciate the comparative serenity that falls on the city's neighbourhoods. Picture it – walking, cycling or riding your moped around with no trucks, no minivans, far fewer taxis, cars, and motorbikes.

For me, spending *Tet* in Saigon is not about visiting 'flower street,' which these days is a huge tourist attraction during the holiday, or visiting pagodas and temples, many of which draw scores of Vietnamese, who come to pray for peace and prosperity through the new lunar year.

The city's transformation is perhaps hard to imagine for those who have never lived here or visited. But for the guts of a week, an overrun, aspiring megalopolis – routinely referred to as one of the most dynamic cities in the world, and also a place where the pollution readings are now considered by the World Health Organisation as alarming – gets to catch its breath. The construction, the consumption, the commotion, much of it fades away, and when the big, brash business hub steps aside, a softly spoken Saigon comes back into focus.

I feel like that's a sight to behold and worth sticking around for, but don't get me wrong – I would never try to convince any fellow residents to consider staying in town for *Tet* in the future. The absence of each and every excursionist is part of the charm of the city during *Tet* (and, seriously, all the best bars and restaurants really are closed for at least a week). In the madding crowd's collective wake, the air will clear (a little) and the dust will settle (a lot). It'll be very quiet, and perhaps not so exciting, but lovely, too. As long as the Wi-Fi doesn't conk out.

Saigon's still singing

The Vietnamese have a saying, *cuoi ngua, xem hoa*, which translates to 'ride a horse, look at the flowers.' Idiomatically, it means, if you're not careful to slow down and pay attention, you will see only the general scenery but miss the important details. I think of this expression whenever Vietnam is marking a significant national anniversary and a legion of the world's media gallops through town. Inevitably mesmerised by the number of glitzy skyscrapers and luxury malls they see in a city that was already being billed as a financial centre and a start-up Mecca, visiting reporters on deadline scramble to find ways to highlight that Ho Chi Minh City – an impoverished place in the late seventies and early eighties – has become a 'voraciously capitalistic' hub, where youthful locals aren't bothered with the past because they are too busy trying to make money and have a good time.

A decade ago, I recall that the *New York Times* sent a reporter to gauge the mood of one such anniversary. At a fancy rooftop bar, the visiting journalist promptly found someone to encapsulate the above snapshot – a young female tech entrepreneur in a black cocktail dress, sipping on a beer and puffing on a hookah. 'Who cares?' she said when he asked for her thoughts (over the din of 'body-rattling beats') on the anniversary of what Americans still call the 'Fall of Saigon.' The young woman was actually a very accomplished personality in the startup world, but she was made to sound like a vacuous Valley girl. History? Like, *whatever*.

There is no denying that Ho Chi Minh City is a place where people come to make money and where many folks like to party. But an alternative take, one based purely on some of the people I was hanging out with a decade ago, could have presented another reality. Around the same time, I had randomly discovered Nguoi Saigon ('Saigonese People'), a small live music venue and vintage-themed cafe, housed in a three-floor modernist building, not so far from the Saigon Opera House.

In those days, one of the owners of Nguoi Saigon was a woman called Bee. She was a self-taught, and highly sought after, technical analyst of the stock market, who never seemed to be at her office. She and some friends (either music lovers or musicians) ran Nguoi Saigon as a passion project. A far cry from the clubby beats of the rooftop bars, a night out at Nguoi Saigon was closer to what I imagine a folk club in New York's Greenwich village might have been like in the early 1960s. Twice a week, a hushed, respectful and intergenerational audience came to listen to bolero music, often referred to as 'pre-1975' music (i.e. before reunification) or *nhac vang* ('yellow music'). A decade ago, at Nguoi Saigon, I watched two dapper singers – one from the Mekong Delta in the southwest of Vietnam and one from a northern province right by the Chinese border – take turns crooning heart-rending ballads to a rapt audience. Some were wiping away tears, and, well, some were swiping away on their phones. But the atmosphere was sincere and affecting. When I pointed out to Bee, who comes from Dalat, that she and many of her pals weren't actually *nguoi* Saigon, she said: 'Anyone who loves this city can call themselves Saigonese.'

During the intermission, and after the show, conversations weren't drowned out by tinnitus-inducing bass lines, making it possible to have an actual conversation. One evening, I chatted with a guy called Dung, a twenty-three-year-old lawyer from Phan Thiet, a seaside town on the southeastern coast. As I sipped a Saigon beer, Dung nursed a fruit juice while telling me that he'd just co-authored a book, under the pen name Mac Thuy, titled *Saigon Van Hat* ('Saigon's Still Singing'). His goal was to document the lives of singers and musicians who infuse the city with so much of its musicality, not on big stages to huge audiences, but in much more intimate venues or open-air restaurants around town. He had no interest in writing about glamorous pop stars or divas performing at sell-out shows. In his eyes, Saigon is a major city that's more accurately captured with minor chords in humble spaces.

After chatting with Dung, I stepped out onto the balcony and spoke with Nguoi Saigon's resident guitarist, a mellow middle-aged fellow called Huy, who batted away the idea that bolero music might one day disappear. 'Just as Americans will always play the folk music of Woody Guthrie, the Saigonese will always sing these old tunes, and now people from every province in Vietnam sing them, too,' he told me between drags on a cigarette. 'Many of the songs we play at Nguoi Saigon were born at the height of war. So at the worst of times, you can say that we produced the most beautiful music.'

Right on cue, a twenty-year old waitress (a student of economics from the Central Highlands) picked up Huy's Spanish guitar and started to strum a gentle bolero song. When I saw her male colleague listening attentively to the sweet lyrics, something about a lover offering to buy an autumn day for his sweetheart, I had to ask if he would be singing a song, too. 'Nah, bolero isn't for me – I prefer hip-hop,' he said with a shrug.

On another night in Nguoi Saigon, there was no show, but a singalong broke out with a few regulars taking turns on the guitar and singing old sentimental ballads. A Saigonese artist now living in Dalat played a tune by Trinh Cong Son, a much loved and revered musician throughout the land. Born in the Central Highlands, Son later migrated to Saigon, where he made a name as a composer. Some of the songs he wrote in the 1960s have been described as 'anti-war,' which is just another way of saying he was a man who longed for peace in a divided country.

When the artist finished his song, he passed the guitar to me. After listening to a tune by Son, a song by Bob Dylan felt appropriate, so I played 'North Country Girl,' thinking of an old flame (and a-wondering if she remembers me at all). By then enough beer and wine had been consumed for someone to insist that the night had to continue. My greatest fear in such situations is a messy session in a gaudy karaoke bar – the closest thing to kryptonite in my Saigon universe. But, instead, we strolled around the Saigon Opera House and down Dong

Khoi Street to Maxim's, an old-school music venue, where renowned local singers often performed. I can't speak for Maxim's in the here and now but in those days it was a 'dinner and a show' kind of place. Many customers came dressed to the nines and eager to dance – the samba, the foxtrot, the cha-cha-cha, all that jazz.

Not for the first time in Ho Chi Minh City, I found myself in an unexpected place with locals taking the lead and music central to the vibe. I have often thought that the Saigonese are quite like the Irish – they love to gather and tell stories, sing songs, laugh, cry, and drink more beer than any GP would recommend; and the more spontaneous the occasion, the happier everyone seems to be.

On a different night, but in the same area, I popped into Chu Bar, just for a look. It was a small venue that used to be on the ground floor of a gorgeous art deco building on the corner of Dong Khoi and Ly Tu Trong Streets – a few doors down from where a CIA helicopter landed as part of the US-led evacuation, fifty years ago in April 1975, a scene famously captured by the Dutch photographer Hubert van Es.

Many of the veteran musicians that frequently played at Chu Bar were in their sixties, if not seventies, at that time. I had been told that some of them were army veterans who had fought alongside US Marines. They were also key players in the Saigon rock scene in the late sixties and, many decades on, they were still sticking to the rock and roll canon, playing tunes by the likes of Creedence Clearwater, The Doors and Roy Orbison. They took turns playing on stage and entertaining old friends at the bar. It was, as the old euphemism goes, a lively occasion. I stayed for a few tunes, and several beers, and left promising that I'd return, but I never did make it back. At some stage, Chu Bar disappeared and now there's a cafe where it used to be. When I saw it had closed, I felt a predictable pang of regret – why hadn't I popped in more often? I might have ended up on stage jamming with the lads, or at least heard a few yarns from back in the day. It can be tough to keep pushing that kind of business up the hill, even if you love it with all your heart.

Over the years, whenever I have had a chat with the owner of a music venue in Saigon, they have pretty much told me the same thing – they don't do it for the money. Of course, they don't want to *lose* money, and making a few bob would be nice, but what is most important to them is creating a space where music can be heard and where music fans can gather.

Some years ago, I interviewed Tran Manh Tuan, a famous saxophonist who used to run a jazz club, Saxnart, right in the heart of District 1. Tuan is a pure showman, one who knows how to work a crowd. I had already been told that when he eventually arrived, he wouldn't rush to the stage, so it was best to wait for him outside. The band (all skilled practitioners) were running through a few classics while customers, drinking gimlets and margaritas, took turns to ask the staff: '*Is Tuan coming tonight?*' When the Main Man finally showed up, he first burned three sticks of incense at an altar by the door. Then after mouthing an inaudible prayer, he ordered a gin and tonic. All his priorities in order.

'You know I have one of my brother's kidneys inside me and I lost sight in one eye. That's why I have got to give thanks for being here playing jazz every night,' he said. 'I'm a lucky man.'

That night, Tuan told me his parents were both acclaimed performers of *cai luong*, a form of Vietnamese theatre that fuses traditional instrumentation, folk songs and classical drama. 'I have composed a number of songs that represent a new form of fusion that blends Vietnamese melodies and instruments with classical jazz concepts. You're gonna hear some of that tonight,' he said, rising from his stool. But first things first. It was time to give the crowd a little love, so he emptied his glass and stood. Without a word, a waiter duly pulled the door open and Tuan strutted inside to the stage, where he launched into a spell-binding version of 'Georgia On My Mind' that brought the house down.

Sadly Tuan's District 1 jazz bar didn't last. It was located in an old shophouse on Le Loi Boulevard, which in terms of rent is probably up there with the likes of the Champs-Elysees or 5th Avenue. After enduring a long closure during the pandemic, he understandably cut his losses and shifted operations to the suburbs, where the rent would likely be cheaper. Thankfully, other music venues have since emerged to keep the flame alive and a few old stalwarts like Nguoi Saigon and Yoko are still going. I hope that visitors to the city will continue to see, and hear, for themselves how Saigon is still singing. But sometimes, even as a long-term resident, chance plays a part. Last year, when cycling across town, I turned down an alleyway not far from Tan Dinh Market to get to NEO, a small cafe-bar with a rooftop, where I cooled off with a local beer and watched the sunset. It was only when I was leaving that I spotted two guitars hanging on the wall. Without much persuasion, the moustachioed *bao ve* (security guard) took one down and sang me an old tune, one that Saigonese often sing at *Tet*: 'Spring goes, spring comes. Let the world be full of nostalgia.'

And after that? Well, not for the first time in Ho Chi Minh City, I returned to the general scenery – a melody in my ears, hope in my swelling heart, a smile on my face. All the important details.

Epilogue: The longing hits home

About twenty-three years ago, I returned to Dublin, flying out of Hanoi on a one-way ticket but fully intending to return. Behind me I had left the bulk of my belongings: some mildewy books; two cases of bootlegged CDs and a guitar; the city's shittiest (read: least cared for) 125cc Minsk motorbike; and all of my tall-man-in-Asia clothes, mostly purchased at the 'Russian shop' – the only store in town that stocked big sizes – or, more regrettably, tailored in the tourist town of Hoi An, in Central Vietnam, which is one way of telling you I often looked like a man who got dressed in the dark.

It was summertime when I arrived and most Dubliners were living it up. Those were the 'Celtic Tiger' years (an economic boom that transformed Ireland's reputation as the poor cousin of Western Europe). Thanks partly to a property bubble that would one day burst, the town appeared to be flush with money. Many of my peers had spent time abroad after university but most of them had now moved back for good. After an uninterrupted two-and-a-half-year stint in Vietnam, I was feeling a bit out of place on the green, green grass of home, which looked the same, but didn't *feel* the same anymore. As I reacquainted myself with old pals and relatives, I was repeatedly told that I was speaking with a wayward accent. This, I realised later, was mainly a result of being an English teacher of beginner students, but also partly from having a girlfriend from Hai Duong (a city not far from Hanoi) and many French friends. As none of the above could understand Irish vernacular or idioms, I had become well-practiced at streamlining my banter and talking slowly enough to be understood. As a result, my speaking voice kept tuning into some oddly Antipodean frequencies. The more alcohol I drank, the more scrambled my accent apparently became. I couldn't hear it myself but one of my best buds told me, with evident concern, I sounded like Lloyd Grossman, still probably the most hurtful thing anyone has ever said to me; and a woman I knew from college asked how long I'd been living in Australia. There is nothing more unsettling than having your identity questioned in your homeland. But it can also, inadvertently, clarify where it is you want to be. I returned to Hanoi with tremendous relief but also excitement, as though I were running back to a lover.

I have never tried to leave Vietnam but, that summer, I certainly got a whiff of how hard it must be for anyone, be they a local or a foreigner, to do so. Without a clear sense of what exactly I was missing about my life in Hanoi, I soon found myself itching (almost literally) to get back, even though I couldn't really explain why to anyone who asked ... The singular pleasure of sitting on the side of the road, drinking iced coffee or cheap beer and riding around on a motorbike (that broke down, on average, once a week) in Hanoi can be hard to convey to those who haven't experienced such simple activities for themselves.

The go-to cliche is that Vietnam and its way of life (whichever 'way of life' you choose there), gets under your skin. The expression implies it can make an addict out of us, and I'm sure many 'departees' have felt like they were experiencing withdrawal symptoms, subconsciously, or consciously, yearning for the joyous clamour of an average Vietnamese street, or the freedom they felt when they were living here. They might have grown to hate the traffic in Hanoi or Saigon, only to find themselves wishing, while stricken with commuter fatigue in a bus or a subway, that they were buzzing around on a motorcycle among it all. Nowadays, whenever I'm away from Saigon for a few weeks, I begin to pine for the place – the fizzing energy of its main roads, the quaint and quotidian rhythms of the back streets, the innumerable cafes, the music (maybe not the karaoke), the chance encounters that occur seemingly everywhere I go, the stories I hear and all of the food I can eat along the merry way. Even Saigonese that disliked the wet season may find themselves, when in a foreign land, longing to be back in the city on a rainy day.

The Portuguese have a good word for this kind of intense longing. *Saudade* describes 'an emotional state of melancholic or profoundly nostalgic longing for a beloved yet absent something or someone,' – a definition that might trigger something in those who have left, or tried to leave Vietnam only to come rushing back months, or even years later. Sometimes it seems like the ones who have left are the ones who love Hanoi and Saigon the most; and even for those who lived here for a relatively short time, Vietnam often seems to have a disproportionate hold on their memories. Of all the countries where they have lived, it's the place they talk, and think, and dream about the most. They carry it in their hearts. They're never without it. Wherever they go, Vietnam goes too.

Over the years, whenever I have penned nostalgic pieces about living in Vietnam, old friends (and people I have never met, too) write to me and share the yearning they feel for Hanoi or Saigon, no matter where they are now – Sydney, San Francisco, Washington, Paris, Tokyo, Singapore, Cape Town, or the Ho Chi Minh City suburb of District 7 …

One friend, who returned to the UK many moons ago, told me that after a solid day's drinking in the middle of a summer heatwave, he'd wandered alone – his friends having disappeared into the Underground and all headed home before 11pm – through Camden Town, when he spotted a Vietnamese restaurant that shone in his eyes like a beacon. The afternoon had begun with him gushing to his friends about life in London. The abundance of resplendent architecture, the parks, the *proper* pubs, the *proper* bookshops, the multiculturalism with every-possible-cross-cultural-identity seemingly accounted for. Even the hard-nosed geezers were more sound than he remembered. But spotting the Vietnamese restaurant, he felt it kick in. That *longing*. That how-can-I-live-without-you anguish. Like someone who has suddenly realised that their ex was the love of his or her life and has to tell them. So, he rushed in the door, grabbed a booth and started speaking (intermediate level) Vietnamese to a waiter, who turned out to have been born in Croydon to Chinese parents. But the owner

... ah-*ha!* ... she was Vietnamese, so my mate cooed her over with his best *chi oi!* ('hey, older sister') to order his *pho* but she was from the south of Vietnam and didn't seem to think much of his Hanoi accent and northern vernacular, so she answered him in Londonised English and scooted away. After a few minutes of sitting in solitude, all the pints he'd drunk that day came home to roost. By the time his (bang average, overpriced) bowl of noodles arrived, he was sobbing.

Plenty of folk I know have taken leave of Vietnam with at least one plan for dealing with the withdrawals to come – they flew to their homeland, or wherever they went next, with half a dozen bags of robusta coffee and an old-school drip filter, the one that sits on top a classic *ca phe den* or *ca phe sua*. Every morning, in some cases for many years, they'd sipped on an iced coffee, daydreaming as they watched the traffic, hypnotised by the minutiae of day-to-day life that transfixes us all in Hanoi and Saigon. They were almost hardwired to start the day with a Vietnamese-style coffee and couldn't imagine living without it. So, after reluctantly packing their bags and arriving for a farewell-drinks session at some streetside beer venue, they'd proudly announced how they'd purchased a few kilos of robusta to help ease the pain of separation. Usually there would have been some helpful discussion, led by sympathetic friends, about the importance of making sure they get the ice just right, as if that were the key to it all, and as if life were that simple …

Some years back, when I visited one repatriated Irishman who had lived in Hanoi for a spell, starting each and every single day with a couple of iced coffees, I pointed out the old filter he'd brought back with him. It was rusting away on his kitchen windowsill, not gone, but certainly forgotten. He then opened a cabinet to reveal he'd hardly put a dent in the supplies of robusta coffee that he'd packed in Hanoi on the eve of his departure. When I asked why, he gazed into his small, suburban garden, more of a yard, really, and said with a shrug: 'It just doesn't taste the same here. I mean – how could it?'

GLOSSARY

Ca phe sua da – an iced coffee

Served with a generous spoonful of condensed milk in a glass packed with ice, *ca phe sua da* is a rather sweet concoction. For older generations of Saigonese it's still the most popular way to enjoy coffee from morning until evening, although some might prefer *ca phe den da* (iced black coffee). On a hot day, a *ca phe sua da* can go down very easily; but be warned, having two in quick succession might leave you with the jitters.

Hem - an alley

Nearly every ward in Ho Chi Minh City is home to a dense network of alleyways. '*Hem* culture' is a huge part of the Saigonese way of life. These alleys are invariably lively places with kids playing games, locals chit-chatting with neighbours or socialising outside their homes. You will often see small businesses – noodle stalls, 'mom and pop stores', small cafes, and much more – operating as well as small temples or shrines down a neighbourhood *hem*. Please note that in Hanoi the word for alley is *ngo* (and an alley off an alley is a *ngach*).

Nhau - to eat, drink and be merry

A near untranslatable word, but to *nhau* basically means to socialise with food and booze for no particular purpose (i.e. it doesn't have to be someone's birthday). You can *nhau* with family members, a bunch of friends or colleagues at a restaurant, a pub (with grub), sitting in a park, or even on the side of the road outside your home. Beer is often the tipple of choice in Ho Chi Minh City, but you can drink any alcohol you wish. For a fuller explanation see 'It's *nhau* or never' on page 37.

Quan nhau - a place to *nhau*

Could be described as a local kind of tavern but is basically a restaurant-bar where you can 'eat, drink and be merry' with family, friends, or colleagues. In Ho Chi Minh City, if you see a lively looking restaurant that spills out onto the street, where groups of boisterous locals are feasting and clinking glasses of beer (often served with ice) then you are looking at a classic *quan nhau*.

Bia - beer

Vietnam has a great appetite for beer, ranking second in Asia (after China) in volume of consumption. In Ho Chi Minh City, bottled beer (*bia chai*) is commonly drunk at local restaurants, Saigon Red and Saigon Special being two of the most popular commercial brews. In the outskirts of the city, you might also spot *bia hoi* (literally, 'fresh beer'), a cheaper and much lighter draft beer that is more popular in Hanoi.

Viet kieu - overseas Vietnamese

'Vietnamese living elsewhere' but also used to describe returning Vietnamese and/or second-generation Vietnamese now living in, or just visiting, Vietnam as expats.

Xe om - motorbike taxi

Refers to the person who offers a motorbike taxi service. Nowadays, ride-hailing apps have largely subsumed this occupation; but on the corner of busy streets, you will still come across some middle-aged or elderly *xe om* (which literally means 'motorbike hug') waiting for a customer. The rate is negotiable but a 2km ride might cost a local VND40,000 (US$1.50).

Con ma – a ghost

Ghosts are deeply embedded in Vietnamese folklore and believed to be everywhere, some happily ensconced at home, others in trees or bodies of water. Those who die without receiving a proper burial become wandering ghosts. For a fuller explanation see 'The life after' on page 113.

Da cau – foot badminton

A sport often seen being played in parks around Ho Chi Minh City. Sometimes players stand in a circle and take turns kicking the shuttlecock to one another – the goal being to keep it in the air for as long as possible. Sometimes you can see doubles matches being played with a net in the middle. Either way, it's always a highly entertaining spectacle.

Dam gio – a death anniversary

An occasion for families (in any part of Vietnam) to commemorate a deceased ancestor on the lunar date of their passing. To express filial piety, a family will typically prepare a house altar with offerings, such as incense, flowers, fruits, food, and votive paper money, before inviting the deceased's spirit to 'return.' The family will then enjoy a meal consisting of dishes the deceased enjoyed during their lifetime. It is a joyous, not mournful, intergenerational affair that breathes life and happiness into the family home.

Tet - Lunar New Year

Short for *Tet Nguyen Dan*, *Tet* refers to the Lunar New Year period, the longest holiday in Vietnam, usually falling between late January and mid-February in the Gregorian calendar. It is typically a time when locals want to be in their ancestral homelands, so in the week before *Tet* begins, Ho Chi Minh City experiences a huge exodus as millions of residents hit the road. This in turn means the city is relatively quiet in its more residential neighbourhoods. The centre of the city will still be busy as tourists and locals flock to 'flower street' (Nguyen Hue Boulevard) or come to see the fireworks on Lunar New Year's Eve. Pagodas and temples will also be crowded as locals come to pray for a prosperous and peaceful new year. For a fuller explanation see '*Tet* is oh so quiet' on page 127.

Dublin-born Connla Stokes is a writer
based in Ho Chi Minh City